LONGMAN BUSINESS ENGLISH SKILLS

Telephoning

KAY BRUCE

Longman

SERIES EDITOR NINA O'DRISCOLL
WITH MARK ELLIS AND ADRIAN PILBEAM

The authors work for Language Training Services

Longman Group UK Limited,
Longman House, Burnt Mill, Harlow
Essex CM20 2JE, England
and Associated Companies throughout the world

Published jointly by Studentlitteratur AB, Lund, Sweden
and Longman Group UK Limited, London, England.

First published 1987
Sixth impression 1989
First published in colour 1992

ISBN 0 582 09306 6

Set in 9/11pt Linotron 202 Helvetica

Produced by Longman Group (FE) Ltd
Printed in Hong Kong

Acknowledgements

We are grateful to the following for their permission to reproduce copyright photographs:

British Telecommunications PLC for page 13, / TeleFocus for page 34; The Image Bank for page 50, / Kaz Mori for page 6 and / Steve Niedorf for page 37; Tony Stone Worldwide for pages 19, 30 and 43.

Cover Photograph by The Image Bank / Jay Freis.

Contents

INTRODUCTION TO THE LEARNER

Telephoning is part of the Longman Business English Skills series. It presents and practises the language used in business situations where the conversation is carried out by telephone. The conversations in each unit take place in familiar situations in different types of company and in different types of offices within those companies. It allows you, as the learner, to both hear and practise the kind of language common to many situations.

Objectives

The book assumes from the start that you have at least a basic general knowledge of English, and that your aim is to improve in an area of more specialized usage. The book has a double function: to allow you to hear and understand fluent conversations and to practise some of the most useful language yourself.

The dialogues

First you are presented with a dialogue, in Part 1 of each unit. You should listen to this as many times as you like to gain a general understanding, but you should not, at this point, read the tapescript. To help you understand the dialogue better, turn first to the *Listening for information* section which contains questions intended to guide you. Next, turn to the *Focus on Language* section, whose purpose is to help you focus on particular language points. In both cases, the objective is to improve your understanding.

Pronunciation

The Pronunciation work is designed to improve your spoken English.

Note the following three points.

contractions – this is when certain words, often auxiliary verbs, are reduced to a single consonant. In every repetition practice in this book, this will be signalled to you by a line underneath the contraction.

liaison – this means the linking of two words by joining the last sound of one, when it is a consonant, to the first sound of the other, when it is a vowel. The two together make a new syllable. This is signalled to you by a half circle underneath the parts of the words to be joined.

stress – some words in a sentence are more important than others: and within those words, there is always one syllable which carries stress, or the main accent. This is signalled to you by a circle showing you which syllable to pronounce more strongly.

Vocabulary Words which are important to the theme of a unit, and which might also be new to you, can be found in the glossary at the end of each unit. There is also a general glossary of useful telephoning expressions on page 80.

The activities This book is designed above all for the student studying alone without the aid of a teacher, and this becomes especially apparent in Part 2 of each unit, where the objective is to give you extensive practice at speaking through a series of Activities. The objective of many of these activities is to simulate a dialogue. Because you will very often be working alone, rather than with a teacher who could provide a response, you will find the other half of the conversation on the cassette. You should prepare yourself to answer or to ask questions from the information in your book and then you should try to 'hold a conversation' with the cassette, speaking in the spaces provided. If you are working alone and without the use of a language laboratory, you can add to the value of this activity by using a second cassette recorder and a blank tape and recording yourself doing each exercise. You can then compare your versions with the ones on the cassette.

The key The key contains the tapescripts and answers. When you have finished Part 1 of each unit, you can read the script while listening to the dialogue. The answers to the Practices and Activities follow the tapescripts. Remember that the answers to the Activities are *suggested* student responses. Yours could be different. However, the versions in the answer section can be used as models.

Approach The cassette recorder gives you great flexibility. In particular, you are able to replay a dialogue or part of a dialogue as many times as you wish.

Do not be afraid to refer to the scripts to help you, if you find the dialogue too difficult. You may want to do this quite a lot, especially in the early stages.

If you take this approach, and do not use the book and cassette as a testing device, you will find that as you progress through the units your understanding and ability to respond correctly will improve dramatically.

1 Getting through, introducing yourself and taking messages

PART 1

The object of this part of the unit is to present ways of getting through to the person you wish to speak to, and of introducing yourself.

Background

You are going to hear Steve Newman, manager of a small company speaking to the switchboard operator in a large office block in London which is shared by many companies. He then speaks to an administrative assistant in a company which provides service offices.

Steve Newman's company is at present based in a London suburb, but would like to move to central London in order to be better placed to take on more business.

Listening for information

Listen to the conversation and use the memo to record the relevant details you think would be noted down by the administrative assistant at Victoria Holdings.

Victoria Holdings Ltd

Memo

Date ________________

To ________________

________________ called

Time ________________

Caller's number is

____

Message

____

____

____

From ________________

Check your memo with the version in the key

Focus on Language

Listen to the conversation again and write down phrases that correspond to the list of purposes below. Some have been done as examples.

	PHRASE	PURPOSE
Conversation between the switchboard operator and Steve Newman.	1 *I'd like to speak to someone about …*	Giving the reason for the call.
	2 ______________________	Offering to get the right person.
	3 *They're the people that deal with it.*	Saying they are in charge, or responsible for it.
	4 ______________________	Asking the caller if he will wait.
	5 ______________________	The caller is showing he is prepared to wait.
	6 ______________________	The operator is explaining the connection has been made.
Conversation between Steve Newman and Charles Hughes the administrative assistant.	7 *Victoria Holdings …*	Answering by giving the name.
	8 *Could I have the name of the company, please?*	This is a polite way of asking for information.
	9 ______________________	The assistant wants to know how to write the name.
	10 *May I have your name?*	This is a polite way of asking the caller's name.
	11 ______________________	The assistant promises to give the information to the right person.
	12 ______________________	Asking if the person can be contacted later.

13 *I'll get Michael Green to call you back. . .* — The assistant promises action.

Check your answers in the key.

14 *Thank you for your call.* — Closing the conversation.

PRACTICE 1 In the following conversation, choose the most suitable response.

A Hello, is that accounts?

B Yes, *it is./I am.* (1)

A I'd like to speak to Sara Adams, please.

B *I am/This is* (2) Sara Adams.

A Hello, my name is Peter Brown, from Pacesetters. *I call/I'm calling* (3) about a bill we sent you.

B Oh, you should speak to my colleague, Roger Simons. I'll put you through to his extension.

A Thank you.

B The line's busy. *Are you holding?/Will you hold?* (4)

A Yes, *I am./I will.* (5)

B I'm afraid the line is still busy. *Would/Could* (6) you give me your number and *I/I'll* (7) ask him to call you *again/back?* (8)

A Yes, certainly. It's 56-89839.

B Thank you. Goodbye.

A Goodbye.

Check your answers in the key.

Language Summary This section draws attention to some of the language used in the dialogue.

	EXAMPLE	COMMENT
Will	*I'll put you through.* *I'll hold on.* *I'll pass this information on.* *I'll get him to do that.* *Will you hold?* *Who'll be able to help you?*	*Will* is used in an immediate reaction, in order to *offer* or *promise* to do something for the caller. When speaking we usually use the contraction (*'ll*), although not at the beginning of a question.

Get	*I'll get him to do that/to ring you back.*	*Get* is a commonly used verb in English: here, it means *I'll* ***ask*** *him to. . .*
Prepositions	*I'll put you* ***through to*** *Victoria Holdings.* *Can he ring you* ***back****?* *I'm interested* ***in*** *renting office space.*	Notice the prepositions are part of the verb.
Telephone numbers	01-449-8927	Notice that we usually say "double four".

PRACTICE 2 **Pronunciation**

Listen to the cassette and repeat the phrases, without the aid of the book. Then listen and repeat with the book, or after having looked at it.

PHRASE

1 *I'd like to speak to someone about renting office space, please.*
2 *Will you hold?*
3 *I'll hold on.*
4 *Can I help you?*
5 *I'm interested in renting office space.*
6 *Could you spell that name for me, please?*
7 *May I have your name?*
8 *and your number?*
9 *01-449-8927.*
10 *I'll pass this information on.*
11 *Can he ring you back?*
12 *Yes, certainly.*
13 *I'll get Michael Green to call you back.*
14 *Thank you for your call.*

PART 2

In this part you are going to practise speaking to a switchboard operator and introducing yourself.

In all four Activities you will hear only one side of the conversation. **You** must act out the other side, by speaking aloud when it is your turn.

ACTIVITY 1 You call a computer company called Zanek Computers. You want to know about their Triple X microcomputers. Speak to the switchboard operator. Try to use some of the language you've already heard and studied.

Compare your version with the model version in the key. It is on the cassette.

ACTIVITY 2 The switchboard operator at Zanek Computers has put you through to the Sales Department. When the Sales Assistant asks you questions, you should use the following information in your answers. You are a potential customer.

Your name: Helen Brown
Your company: Bartlett & Company
Your number: 927-5651
You want information about: Triple X micro-computers for use in the office

Compare your version with the model version in the key. It is on the cassette.

Now play the cassette and reply appropriately, using the information above.

ACTIVITY 3 You are the secretary in the accounts department of a large company and are responsible for receiving calls and putting the caller through to the right person. Here, a caller wishes to speak to your colleague, Judith Roberts. At first, Judith's number is engaged, but it rings the second time. You are the secretary: speak to the caller.

Compare your version with the model version in the key. It is on the cassette.

ACTIVITY 4 You receive a call about your company's range of video cassette recorders. You are responsible for sales of the Standard recorder, and your colleague, Geoffrey White, is responsible for the Deluxe Model. So when you receive the call, deal with the enquiry:

- give the name of your department (Sales)
- find out if the caller wants Standard or Deluxe
- make a note of the caller's name, the name of their company and the telephone number
- tell the caller you'll give the information to Geoffrey White

Compare your version with the model version in the key. It is on the cassette.

Glossary

switchboard operator the person who works on the switchboard, which is the central point for all calls coming into the company

service offices offices where all the furniture, telephone and services such as photocopying and typing, are provided

deal with to be in charge of, or responsible for, something

put through to someone, usually the operator, connects or passes you to someone else

hold, hold on wait, don't go away

pass on to give or transmit information to the right person

2 Recorded messages

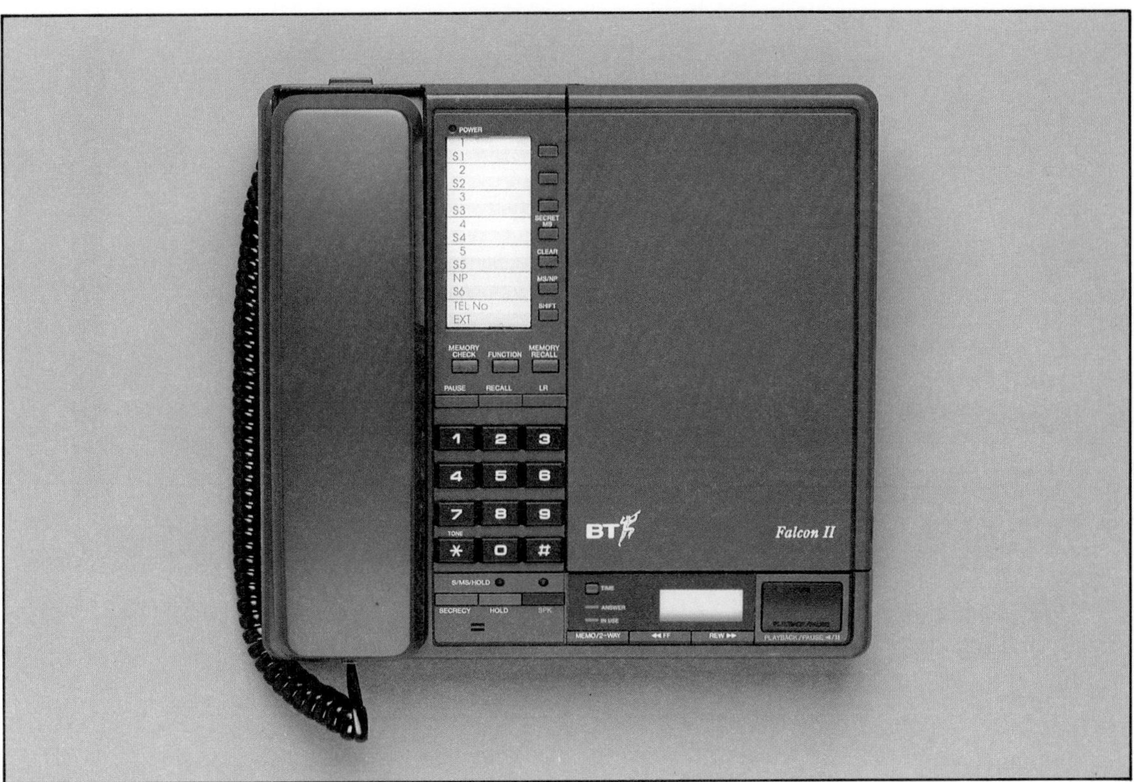

PART 1

This part of the unit will present examples of recorded messages on answerphones and will give practice in leaving your own messages.

Background

Lionel Webster works as a buyer in a busy import/export office in London. He often receives phone calls from all over the world from brokers with offers of cargo for sale.

You are going to hear a broker leaving a message on Webster's answerphone concerning the arrival of the ship carrying his cargo.

Listening for information

Note the following details while you are listening to the message for the first time.

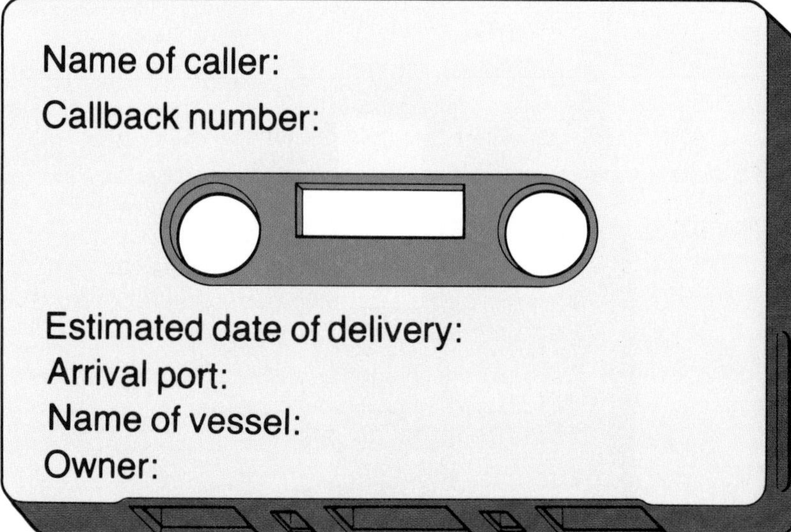

Name of caller:
Callback number:
Estimated date of delivery:
Arrival port:
Name of vessel:
Owner:

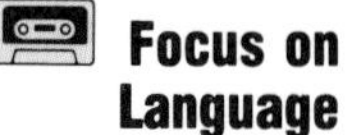

Focus on Language

Now listen to the cassette again and answer the following questions.

1 What phrases does Webster use to:
   a introduce himself?
   b explain his absence?
   c give instructions to the caller?
   d thank the caller?
2 Webster explains he will return soon; what words does he use instead of *return* and *soon*?
3 How does Bonner introduce himself?
4 What are the two phrases he uses when he spells words?
5 What phrase does he use to give the reason for his call?
6 When exactly will he call back?
7 Does he want Lionel Webster to do anything?

Check your answers in the key.

Language Summary This section draws attention to some of the language used in the dialogue.

	EXAMPLE	COMMENT
Will	*The vessel will be the* Atheco.	Helmut Bonner uses *will*, to show that the information is definite.
	I'll spell that. *I'll call back with the exact time of arrival.*	He offers or promises to do something very specific.
From	*I'm calling from Hamburg.*	He is giving information about *where*. . .
About	*I'm calling about our next delivery to you.*	. . .and *why* he is calling.

PRACTICE 1 **Pronunciation**

Listen to the next part of the cassette and repeat the phrases without the aid of the book. Then listen and repeat with the book, or after having looked at it.

PHRASE	NOTES
1 *This is Lionel Webster speaking.*	Notice the name is said more slowly, and with more emphasis, than the rest of the phrase.
2 *I'm not in the office at the moment. . .*	Notice how his tone *rises* at the end of the last word.
3 *but I expect to be back shortly.*	Notice how his tone *drops* at the end of the last word.
4 *Please leave your name, number and a message of no more than three minutes, when you hear the signal.* 5 *Thank you for your call.*	Notice the pauses after *name*, *number* and *minutes*.

 **PRACTICE 2** Using the following information, prepare a message as if for an answerphone. Try to use some of the language Lionel Webster used.

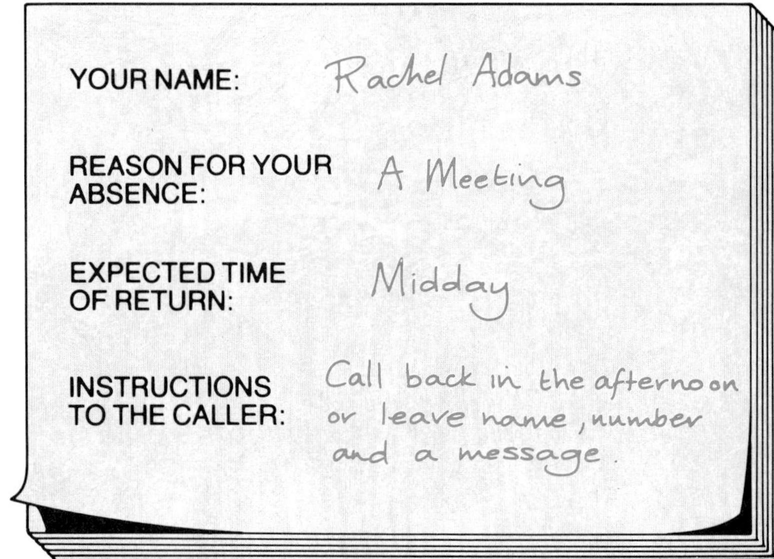

YOUR NAME: Rachel Adams

REASON FOR YOUR ABSENCE: A Meeting

EXPECTED TIME OF RETURN: Midday

INSTRUCTIONS TO THE CALLER: Call back in the afternoon or leave name, number and a message.

Compare your version with the model version in the key. It is on the cassette.

PRACTICE 3 **Pronunciation**

As with Practice 1, listen and repeat without reading, then open your book and do it again.

PHRASE

1 *Helmut Bonner here. That's B.O.N.N.E.R.*

2 *My number is 880-51-01.*

3 *I'm calling about our next delivery to you.*

4 *The vessel will be the "Atheco" – I'll spell that.*

5 *I'll call back within the next two days.*

NOTES

Compare this with the way Lionel introduces himself – it's quicker and more informal.

When saying telephone numbers, people often say "double-eight" rather than "eight-eight".

PART 2

This part of the unit gives you further practice in understanding and leaving messages.

ACTIVITY 1

a Listen to the recorded information concerning an international mining congress. While you are listening, note the main details.

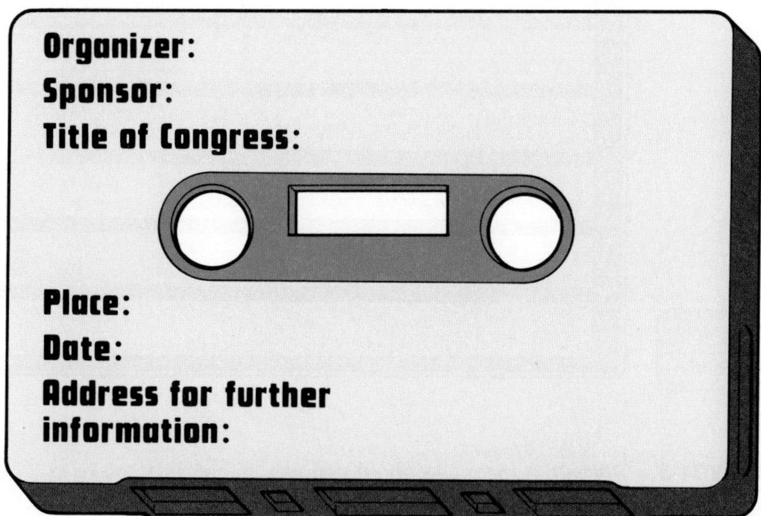

Organizer:
Sponsor:
Title of Congress:
Place:
Date:
Address for further information:

Check your answers in the key.

b Having decided to attend the Congress, phone your colleague in Buenos Aires. Prepare the following message for her answerphone. (You could try recording it on a blank cassette or write it.)

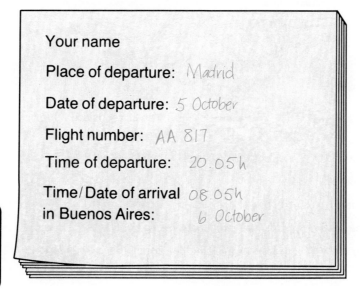

Your name

Place of departure: Madrid

Date of departure: 5 October

Flight number: AA 817

Time of departure: 20.05h

Time/Date of arrival in Buenos Aires: 08.05h 6 October

Compare your version with the model version in the key. It is on the cassette.

ACTIVITY 2 Listen to this recording on a travel agent's phone. It gives updated information on flights an airline company has to offer to the USA over the next few days. Make a note of the details.

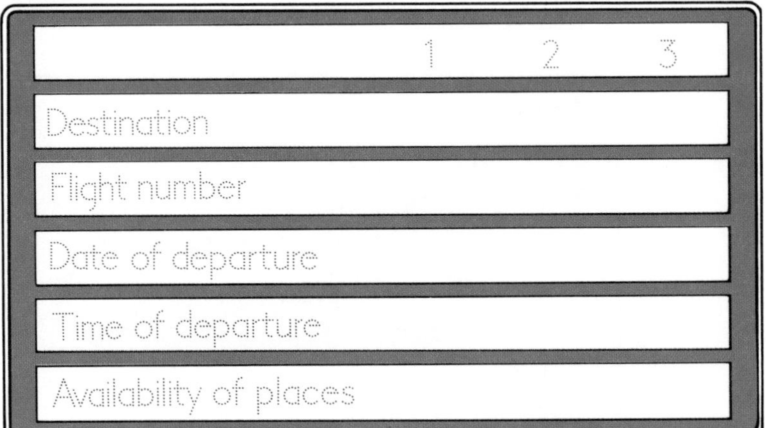

	1	2	3
Destination			
Flight number			
Date of departure			
Time of departure			
Availability of places			

Check your answers in the key.

ACTIVITY 3 Prepare a message about yourself, either at home or in the office.

You should include the following language:

This is. . .

. . .out at the moment.

I'll be back. . .

Please leave. . .

I'll call you. . .

Compare your version with the one given for Practice 2.

Glossary

broker someone who does business, especially buying, for other people

cargo a specific amount of goods or merchandise

vessel usually, a ship

delivery taking goods to the door of the buyer

freight any goods, or merchandise being transported

take off when a plane leaves the ground: the opposite is **to land**

3 Fixing appointments

PART 1

The objective of this unit is to present language commonly used on the phone when arranging meetings and fixing appointments.

Background

You will first hear a conversation between Lisa Alexander, the manager of a small company *Wool Touch,* and her bank manager, Mr Sanchez. *Wool Touch* is a young company specializing in woollen and woven products. Lisa Alexander is interested in investing in new equipment, for which she is hoping for financial help from her bank, the General Union.

Listening for information

Before you listen, read the following message. It was addressed to the credit manager of General Union Bank, Dominic Sanchez, by his secretary.

GENERAL UNION BANK PLC

To: Mr Sanchez

Lisa Alexander CALLED FROM

"Wool Touch" COMPANY

DAY: today

TIME: 11.45 am

S/HE:
- LEFT NO MESSAGE
- WILL CALL BACK
- WANTS YOU TO CALL BACK ON:
- 27854
- LEFT THIS MESSAGE

Wants info on credit facilities re purchase of new equipment

Now as you listen to the conversation, fill in the details of the appointment in Mr Sanchez's desk diary. Also, complete the note Mr Sanchez makes to himself under the heading IMPORTANT.

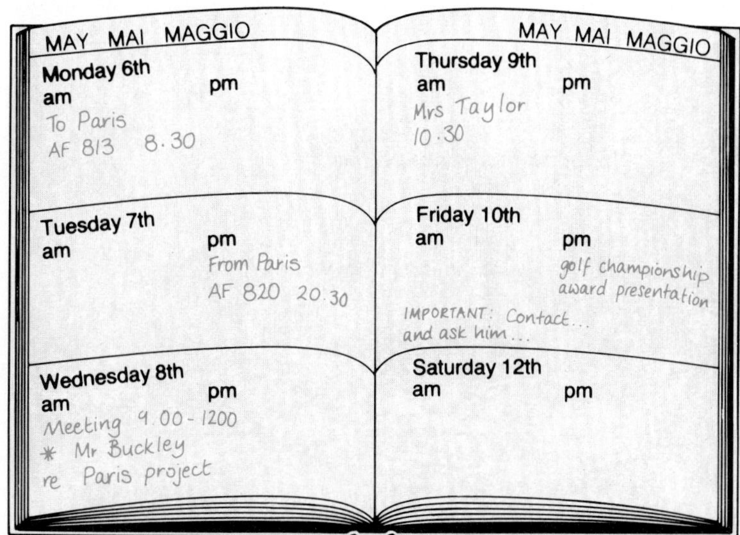

MAY MAI MAGGIO
Monday 6th
am
pm
To Paris
AF 813 8.30
Tuesday 7th
am
pm
From Paris
AF 820 20.30
Wednesday 8th
am
pm
Meeting 9.00-1200
* Mr Buckley
re Paris project
MAY MAI MAGGIO
Thursday 9th
am
pm
Mrs Taylor
10.30
Friday 10th
am
pm
golf championship
award presentation
IMPORTANT: Contact...
and ask him...
Saturday 12th
am
pm

Check with the diary in the key.

Focus on Language

Listen to the conversation again and, as in Unit 1, write down phrases that correspond to the list of purposes below. Some have been done already.

Conversation between Mr Sanchez and Ms Alexander's secretary

PHRASE	PURPOSE
1 ______________________	This is how Mr Sanchez introduces himself. Notice he doesn't say *I am*.
2 *And what is it about?*	This is one question you can use to discover the reason for a call.
3 ______________________	Mr Sanchez received a message telling him to call Ms Alexander: this is how he gives his reason for the call.

Conversation between Mr Sanchez and Ms Alexander

4 ______________________________

This shows doubt and is a request for more information from Ms Alexander.

5 *Would you like to come in and see me. . .?*

Mr Sanchez is inviting Ms Alexander to visit him at the bank.

6 *I think that would be best.*

Ms Alexander is showing she agrees with the suggestion.

7 *Can we fix an appointment now?*

Or *make an appointment.*

8 ______________________________

I'll get my diary would be another way to say this.

9 *Does tomorrow morning suit you?*

This is a way of asking if a particular day is convenient.

10 ______________________________

This is a fairly informal way of suggesting a time.

Check your answers in the key.

11 ______________________________

She is showing she agrees with the suggestion.

Language Summary

This section draws attention to some of the structures used in the dialogue.

Questions inviting affirmation or agreement

1 Tag questions

EXAMPLES

It was about credit facilities, wasn't it?

You do realize that in either case we would charge a commitment fee, don't you?

Q *You don't require any other facilities, do you?*
A *No, I don't, thank you.*
Q *There were some other problems, weren't there?*
A *Yes, that's right.*

COMMENT

Negative endings are used when you expect or want someone to say *yes.*

Positive endings are used when you expect the answer to be *no.*

2 Other questions where the speaker is asking for confirmation or agreement

I believe you're planning on investing in new equipment. Is that right?

Shall we say ten?

PRACTICE 1 These are some of the questions asked by Dominic Sanchez and Lisa Alexander during their meeting the following day.

Complete them with the appropriate question tag (look at the examples).

Decide who the speaker was in each case.

	Speaker: Sanchez	Speaker: Alexander
1 *A loan would have a fixed rate of interest, ________ ?*	☐	☐
2 *Investing in new equipment is part of your overall expansion plan, ________ ?*	☐	☐
3 *Your end-of-year figures showed quite a healthy profit, ________ ?*	☐	☐
4 *You're planning on taking on new people, ________ ?*	☐	☐
5 *I could decide to go for an overdraft, ________ ?*	☐	☐

Check your answers in the key.

PRACTICE 2 As well as using a question tag, we can use the phrase such as *Is that right?* Use this phrase to construct fairly formal questions, beginning with one of these phrases:

I've been told. . .

I believe. . .

As I understand it,. . .

I've heard that. . .

Example: *You're planning on investing in new equipment.*

I believe you're planning on investing in new equipment, is that right?

1 General Union Loan Scheme: designed to help small companies.

2 Loan: more appropriate than overdraft.

3 Wool Touch: expanding into American market.

4 Wool Touch: won design award last year.

Compare your four questions with the model questions in the key. They are on the cassette.

PRACTICE 3 **A** When fixing the time of their meeting, Mr Sanchez used the fairly informal *Shall we say – ?*. We can use this to agree on any aspects of a meeting, as well as many other details, for example:

lunch *Shall we say lunch?*

Make two sentences like this one, using these words:

1 Tuesday, Commodore Hotel
2 12%, 18 months

B Now that you have seen some formal and informal ways of fixing appointments, look at the following questions and decide which they are. The first two have been done for you.

1. *Does tomorrow suit you?* formal
2. *Shall we say ten?* informal
3. *Would Tuesday be convenient?*
4. *How about Tuesday?*
5. *May I suggest Tuesday rather than Monday?*
6. *Do you think Tuesday's OK?*

Check your answers in the key.

PRACTICE 4 **Pronunciation**

Listen to the next part of the cassette and repeat the phrases, without the aid of the book. Then, listen and repeat with the book, or after having looked at it.

PHRASE

1. *Who's calling?*
2. *It's Mr Sanchez.*
3. *And what is it about?*
4. *I'm returning her call.*
5. *Thank you for calling me back so promptly.*
6. *It was about credit facilities, wasn't it?*
7. *I believe you're planning on investing in new equipment is that right?*
8. *Were you thinking in terms of overdraft facilities?*
9. *You do realize that in either case we would charge you a commitment fee, don't you?*
10. *Would you like to come in and see me?*
11. *I think that'd be best.*
12. *Can we fix an appointment now?*
13. *Let me get my diary. Does tomorrow morning suit you? Shall we say ten?*
14. *That's fine by me.*

PART 2

In this part you have further opportunity to practise the language introduced in Part 1.

ACTIVITY 1

You need to arrange a meeting with a colleague, Helen Green. You start your side of the telephone conversation by saying *I'd like to arrange a meeting*. Then continue the conversation using the information in your diary, which shows when you already have appointments.

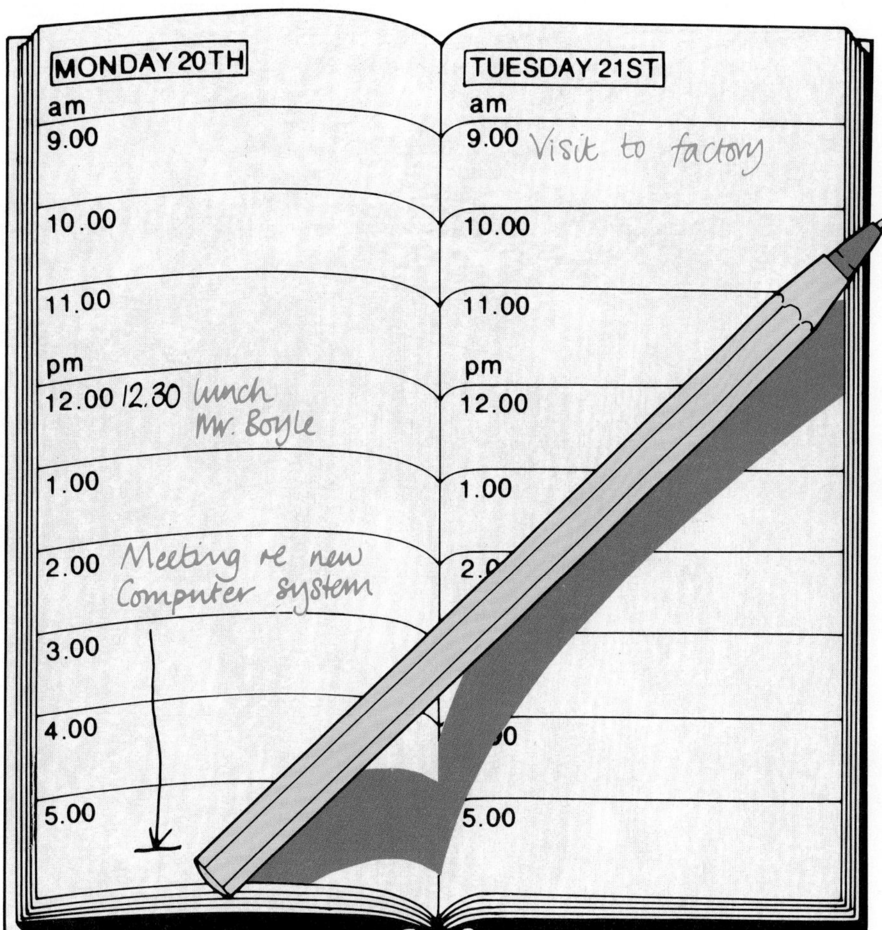

Compare your version with the model version in the key. It is on the cassette.

ACTIVITY 2 You left a message for a colleague, Rafael, asking him to call you back, as you wanted to fix an appointment to see him. When he calls you back, respond appropriately, using the information in your diary. Your diary is not near the phone: you have to get it. Listen to what Rafael says to you and try writing your responses before working with the cassette.

Rafael *Hello this is Rafael. I'm returning your call.*

You . . .

Rafael *Yes, certainly. When for?*

You . . .

Rafael *Wednesday morning. OK. What time?*

You . . .

Rafael *Half past nine suits me. Look forward to seeing you then. Bye.*

You . . .

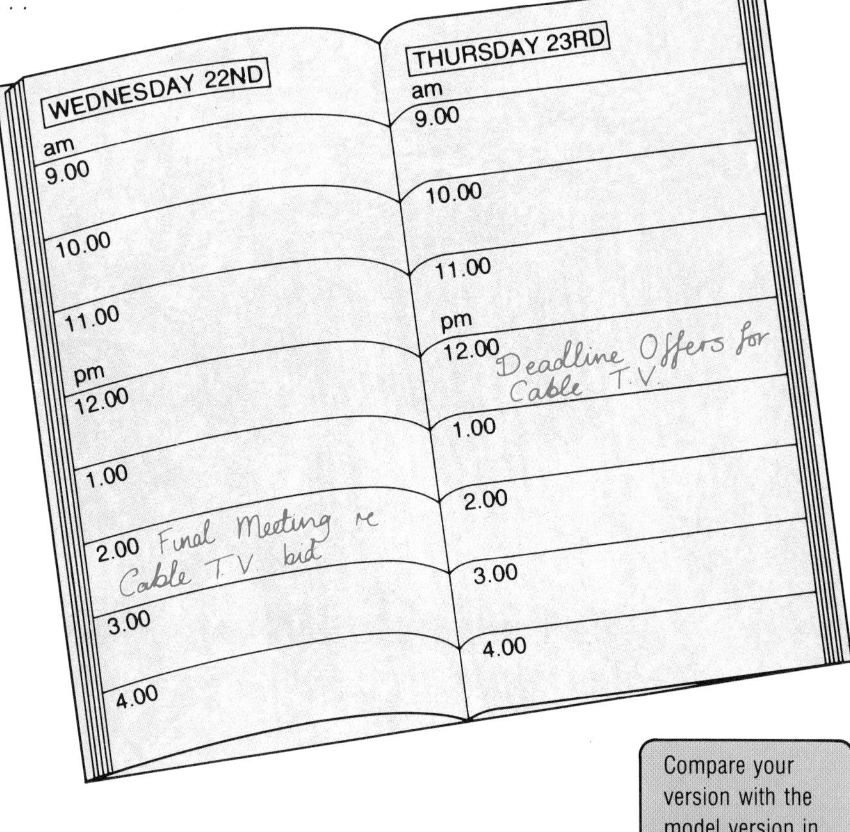

Compare your version with the model version in the key. It is on the cassette.

ACTIVITY 3 Look at this advertisement from a local garage repair shop. Then complete the conversation between a customer, Mr Gilmer, and the garage.

BODY SHOP

HALF PRICE

"Body Shop" offers a full service for your car

If you can bring in your car at short notice, we will guarantee same-day service. A complete service at half the normal price. Just phone for details of how to do it.

This offer is open to everybody **Phone 20958**

Mr Gilmer has already been in touch with Bodyshop, who service people's cars at short notice on days when they find they have a little extra time.

Conversation

Mr Gilmer	*Hello, 47580?*
Bodyshop	*Hello, Mr Gilmer?*
Mr Gilmer	_______ (1)
Bodyshop	_______ *Bodyshop repairs.* (2)
Mr Gilmer	_______ *(3)*
Bodyshop	*Today looks fairly quiet and so we could take your car.*
Mr Gilmer	*Yes, what time?*
Bodyshop	_______ (4)
Mr Gilmer	*Ten o'clock. Yes* _______ (5)
Bodyshop	*Good. See you later.*
Mr Gilmer	_______ (6) *Thank you. Goodbye.*

Compare your version with the version in the key.

ACTIVITY 4 Listen to the telephone conversation between an insurance broker and a potential customer and look at the form at the same time. Which boxes do you think the broker did not tick?

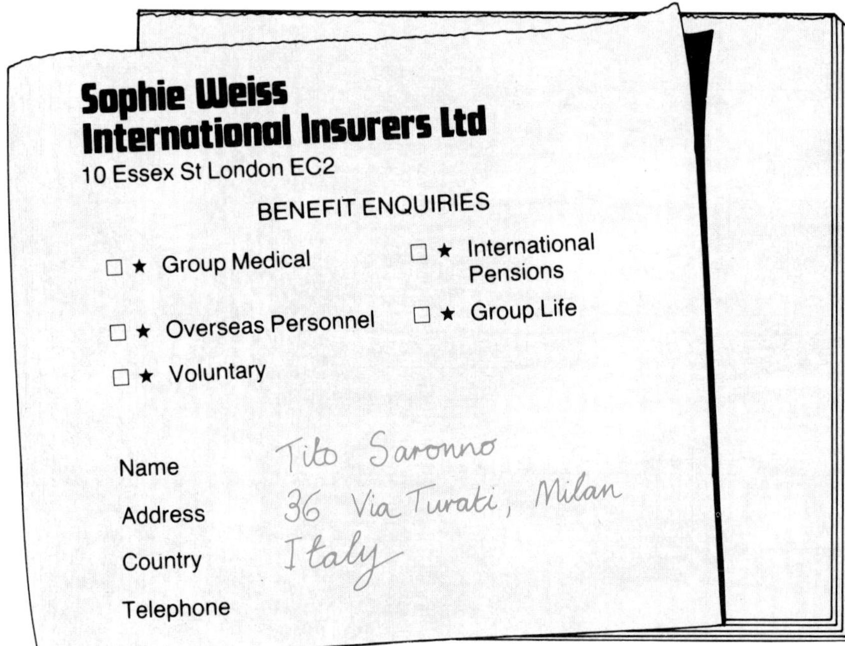

Sophie Weiss International Insurers Ltd

10 Essex St London EC2

BENEFIT ENQUIRIES

- ☐ ★ Group Medical
- ☐ ★ International Pensions
- ☐ ★ Overseas Personnel
- ☐ ★ Group Life
- ☐ ★ Voluntary

Name Tito Saronno

Address 36 Via Turati, Milan

Country Italy

Telephone

Check your answer in the key. Also, check the address on the form. Is it correct?

Glossary

woollen made of wool

woven past participle of to weave – to twist threads over and under each other to make a piece of cloth, etc.

purchase the act of buying

tag something added to the end of a sentence to make it into a question

fee an amount of money charged for a service

overall general, referring to the whole

figures an amount of money stated in numbers

take on to employ

overdraft an amount which exceeds the money you have in the bank

loan a certain sum of money which a bank, etc. agrees to lend you

award prize

deadline the latest date by which something must be done

notice information about something which is going to happen within a certain amount of time

4 Discussing information; changing appointments

PART 1

In this unit you are going to hear language used when you wish to change appointments, and also language which is commonly used when someone you wish to speak to is unavailable.

Background

You are going to hear a conversation between Nils Ekström, a market analyst and Janine Berman, the director of public relations of a European computer company.

Nils Ekström is a specialist in Scandinavian markets. Here he talks to Janine Berman of AKD Computers, a successful company which is nevertheless constantly aware of American competition. AKD are about to launch their latest and most sophisticated personal computer, PAL.

Listening for information

After listening to the conversation, answer these questions.

1 What is the reason for Nils's call?

2 Did he cancel their meeting or just postpone it?

3 Do Nils and Janine agree about the state of the stock market at the moment?

4 From what Nils says about shares, does the company seem to be a good investment at the moment?

5 Does AKD seem to have a promising future?

6 Does Nils appear satisfied by his conversation with Janine?

7 Did he only call about their meeting?

Check your answers in the key.

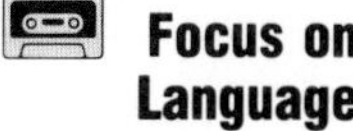

Focus on Language

Listen to the conversation again and write down phrases that correspond to the list of purposes below. Some have been done as examples.

PHRASE	PURPOSE
1 ______________________	Nils uses this phrase to introduce a subject, in this case the meeting.
2 ______________________	Nils is using this phrase to apologise: but it can also be used to introduce anything negative.
3 *You see,*	Nils uses this to start an explanation.

4 ______________________________

Janine is talking about the stock market and uses this phrase to explain what seems to be a contradictory aspect of the current situation.

5 *Hm – the market is bad. . .*

Nils is agreeing with what Janine is saying.

6 ______________________________

Nils is revealing a precise piece of information concerning his plans.

7 *Ah well, that's very interesting,*

Janine is showing her approval.

8 ______________________________

Nils fully agrees with what Janine has said: this is how he shows it.

Check your answers in the key.

Language Summary

This section draws attention to some of the language used in the dialogue.

	EXAMPLE	COMMENT
Afraid	*I'm afraid I won't be able to make it.*	You can use *I'm afraid* and *I'm sorry, but. . .* as a means both to apologise and to introduce negative information.
Will	*I'll be bringing a client.*	*Will* is used with the participle, to indicate an event which is certain.
	I won't be able to make it.	The contraction of *will not* also shows something which is certain.

Have	*I have heard some interesting rumours.*	*Have* is used with the past participle to mean recently.
Make	*Make (our meeting).*	*Make* is used to mean *keep an appointment* or *attend a meeting.*

PRACTICE 1 Use *make* to suggest these times and dates for meetings. You should vary your language as much as possible, and use different structures and phrases in each sentence.

1 10 o'clock
2 Friday
3 next week

Now use *make* to apologise for not being able to keep these meetings:

4 the department meeting
5 the first appointment
6 Friday

Compare your answers with the ones in the key.

PRACTICE 2 **Pronunciation**

Listen to the next part of the cassette and repeat the phrases without the aid of the book. Then listen and repeat with the book, or after having looked at it.

PHRASE **NOTES**

1 *It's about our meeting.*
2 *I'm afraid I won't be able to make it after all.*
3 *Would you like to arrange another date?*
4 *I have heard some interesting rumours about the new PAL.* — Notice the special stress on *have.*
5 *I think we can say that the PAL is very promising.*
6 *Well, actually I'm coming to the AGM.*
7 *I'll look forward to seeing you then.*

PART 2

In Activities 1 and 2 you are going to practise language used when the person you wish to speak to is unavailable. Activity 3 gives you practice in linking items of information together, using words introduced in the unit.

ACTIVITY 1

The two switchboard operators are explaining why they cannot connect callers to the people they want to speak to.

Look at the phrases they use. Which of them are similar in meaning? Can you group the similar phrases into pairs and say how they are similar?

1 . . . *there's no reply.*

2 . . . *she's on a visit to a supplier.*

3 . . . *he's sick today.*

4 . . . *she's on another line.*

5 . . . *he'll be out all day.*

6 . . . *I can't reach him.*

7 . . . *she's with a customer.*

8 . . . *she'll be back tomorrow.*

9 . . . *he's on holiday.*

10 . . . *he's not in the office at the moment.*

Check your answers in the key.

ACTIVITY 2 Look at this page from the appointments book of a doctors' surgery, which gives information about the doctors' activities each morning. Then listen to the cassette. You will hear different patients calling to speak to the doctors. Answer for the receptionist. Give the reason why you cannot put the caller through. Try to use some of the language from Activity 1.

MONDAY 10 AUGUST

	Dr Rogers	Dr Lemon	Dr Willis	Dr Morris	Dr Poole	Dr Nahri
8		Patients			Patients	
9	Hospital visit	Mrs Delaney Mr Ellis	Holiday	Day off	Miss Brice Mrs Ewles	Sick
10		Mr Brown Mr Vincorsi			Mr Brenham Mr Reed	
11		Mrs Naim Miss de Sonza			Mrs Patel Mr Richards	
12		Mr Poirer			Mrs Jones Mr Smith	

Check your version with the model version in the key. It is on the cassette.

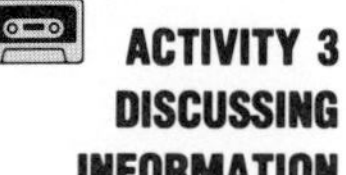

ACTIVITY 3
DISCUSSING INFORMATION

Make sentences about these different economic areas by combining particular facts. In each case, use one of these expressions – *actually, in fact, indeed* – to give the final specific piece of information:

When you have completed the first one, compare your version with the one in the key. It is on the cassette. (Do **not** look at **2** and **3** yet.)

1 French arms sales
1984 total = $6.66 bn.
Double 1983 total
A record

2 Europe: wages linked to prices.
Unemployment grows.
Japan: wages linked to company profits.
Unemployment relatively insignificant.

3 Natural Grain Products started 1970.
President Laurence Ford now a rich man.
Sales = $7 m. last year.

Compare your versions with the ones in the key. They are on the cassette.

Glossary

cancel	to remove, give up
postpone	to move something to a later date
stock market	the place where stocks and shares are bought and sold
shares	the ownership of a company divided into parts which people can invest in
promising	with a lot of potential
look forward to	to anticipate something pleasurable
switchboard operator	calls coming into a company are directed to a central point
switchboard	the operator works here
put a caller through	to connect or to pass a caller
shareholder	a person owning shares in a company
AGM	Annual General Meeting
have a chat	have an informal talk about something

5 Making a booking; repeating and clarifying information

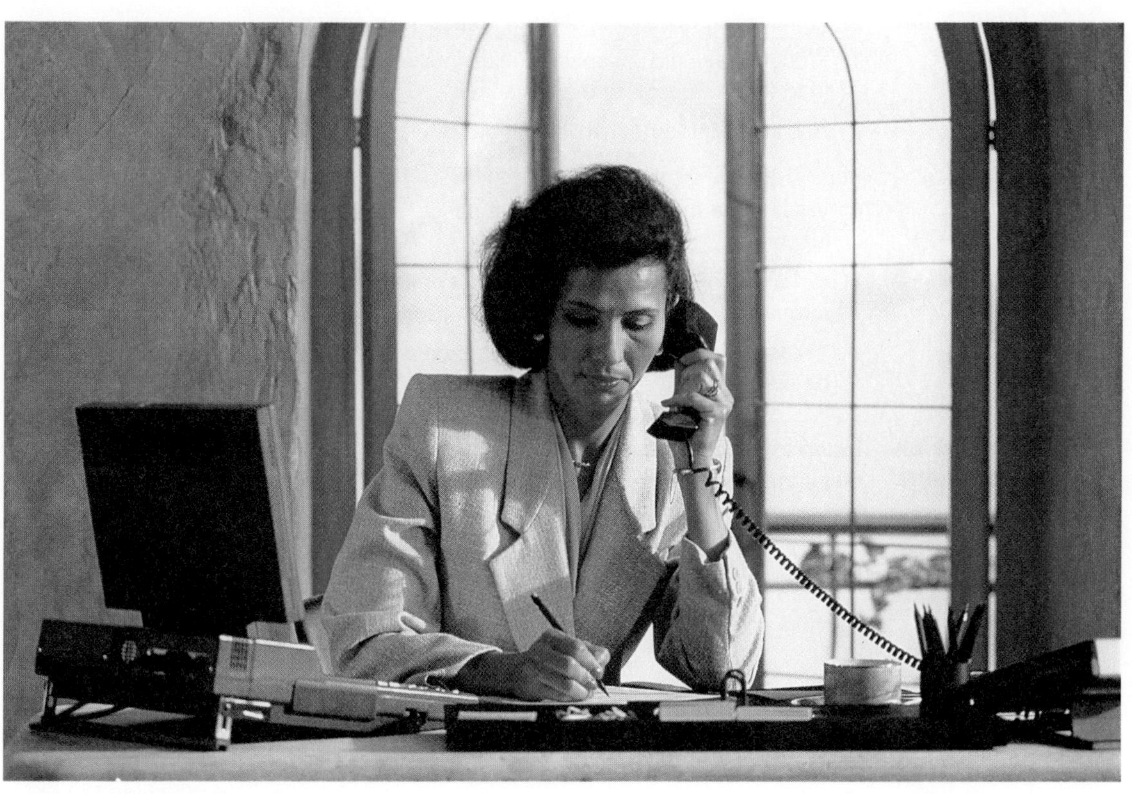

PART 1

The objective of this unit is to present and practise language commonly used when asking for clarification and repetition on the telephone. It also consolidates many of the elements in Units 1 to 4.

Background

Josephine Pinzan is the recently appointed Press Officer in a multinational company. As such, she has a lot of entertaining to do, particularly with journalists, and the standard practice when this is on company premises is to book a private room. Here, she calls Ingrid Bellini, the restaurant manager, to make a booking.

Listening for information

As you listen to the cassette, listen particularly for answers to the following questions. Make a note of your answers.

1 What mistake did Josephine Pinzan make when she first tried to get through to the restaurant?

2 Had Ingrid Bellini heard of her before?

3 Why didn't she understand Josephine Pinzan at first?

4 What is the maximum number of people expected for lunch?

5 What kind of lunch will it be? A buffet or something more formal?

6 At the end of the conversation what details still need to be confirmed?

Check your answers in the key.

Focus on Language

Listen to the conversation again and write down phrases that correspond to the list of purposes below. Some have been done as examples.

PHRASE	PURPOSE
1 ______________________	The person is explaining that it is not the restaurant.
2 *I'll see if I can put you through.*	He is offering to connect her to the restaurant.
3 ______________________	Josephine is apologising for her mistake.
4 ______________________	Mrs Bellini is asking her to repeat her surname.

5 *I'm afraid this is a bad line.*	Mrs Bellini is explaining why she is having difficulty understanding her.
6 ______________________	She is asking her to repeat the day.
7 *I'll let you know definitely later on.*	She is promising to give more precise information later.
8 ______________________	She is asking her to repeat the number of people expected.
9 *I'll have to confirm it.*	She is showing that the details are not yet certain.
10 ______________________	She is asking for more details about what is available for a lunch.
11 ______________________	She is asking her to repeat the choice of desserts.
12 *Could I think about it and call you back?*	She is asking for some time before confirming the details.
13 ______________________	She is agreeing to Josephine's suggestion.
14 ______________________	She is checking that Thursday is OK.
15 *I'll check my bookings...*	She is showing that she needs to confirm the details.
16 ______________________	Josephine is promising to confirm the booking as soon as possible.

Check your answers in the key.

Language Summary

This section draws attention to some of the language used in the dialogue.

	EXAMPLE	COMMENT
Sorry	*Sorry to trouble you.* *Sorry but I didn't catch your surname.*	These are more examples of making apologies.
Get + -ing	*I've got some people coming.*	This is the structure to follow: get + someone + verb-ing.
Did. . .didn't you?	*You did say Thursday was all right, didn't you?*	This is another example of the tag question, used here to check information.

PRACTICE 1 Pronunciation

Listen to the next part of the cassette and repeat the phrases, without the aid of the book. Then, listen and repeat with the book, or after having looked at it.

PHRASE	NOTES
1 *You've got the wrong extension.*	
2 *I'll see if I can put you through.*	
3 *Sorry to trouble you.*	
4 *I didn't catch your surname.*	
5 *How can I help you?*	
6 *I'm afraid this is a bad line.*	
7 *What day did you say?*	Notice the rising intonation
8 *I'll let you know definitely.*	
9 *I'm sorry.*	
10 *Could you repeat how many?*	
11 *I'll have to confirm it.*	
12 *Could you run through the choices?*	

13 *Sorry, soufflé, ice cream or. . .*

Notice the rising intonation

14 *You did say Thursday was all right, didn't you?*

PART 2

In this part you have the opportunity to practise further some of the language presented in Part 1.

ACTIVITY 1 You are making a phone call to a person you have never spoken to before, Mr Bonner. His extension number is 5410. Listen to the cassette and respond. Make sure you get the right person.

Compare your version with the model version in the key. It is on the cassette.

ACTIVITY 2 Listen to the conversation between a salesman and a managing director James Bassett and make a note of the essential details, as if you were the managing director, e.g. name, phone number, etc.

Check your answers in the key.

ACTIVITY 3 Using the information in Activity 2, call the advertising manager Brian Williams and pass the details on. Be ready to repeat any information necessary, as it is a bad line. You should follow these steps:

1 Introduce yourself. Your name is James.
2 Ask if he knows *The Advertiser.*
3 Tell him Simon Stott just rang.
4 Tell him the circulation figure.
5 Ask him to ring Simon Stott and give him the phone number.

Compare your version with the version in the key. It is on the cassette.

ACTIVITY 4 Listen to five telephone calls. How do you respond in each case?

Compare your five responses with the model responses in the key. They are on the cassette.

Glossary

booking	a reservation
entertaining	receiving people and providing food and drink for them
buffet	usually cold food, set out on a long table, self-served
soufflé	a light, airy dish based on beaten eggs
(to) catch	to understand, to hear
starter	the first course
pie	(or tart) either fruit, a dessert, or meat enclosed in pastry and cooked
circulation	the number of copies sold

6 Checking and discussing information

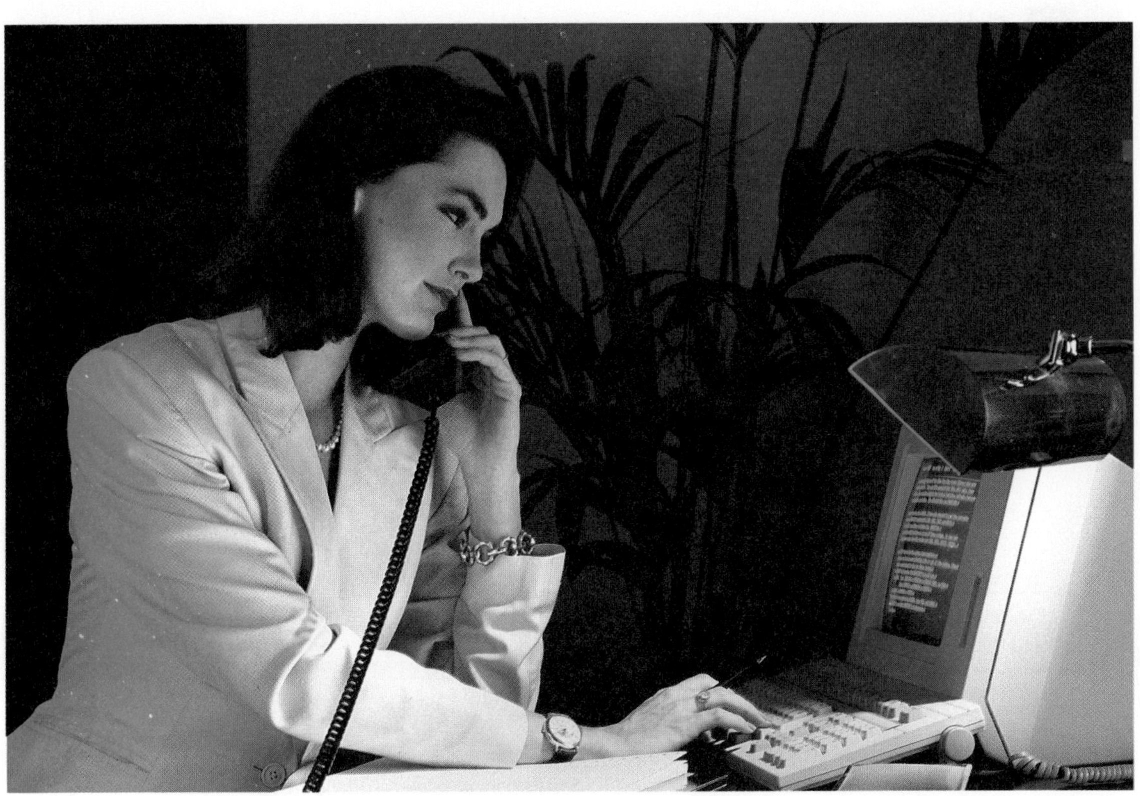

PART 1

In this unit you will hear and practise language which is often used when checking and discussing information. In particular, this involves a lot of questioning.

Background

You are going to hear Hanna Willems, a sales analyst for an oil company in Amsterdam, discussing forecasts with her counterpart, Lewis Brown, at the company's head office in London.

The company deals in oil production and sales and has affiliates all over Europe. Head office and affiliates telephone each other every month to update forecasts of sales.

Listening for information

While you are listening to the cassette for the first time, fill in this chart, which reflects the changing sales figures of different types of oil.

Month: JANUARY	*Forecast*	*Best Estimate*
Heavy Fuel Oil:		
Domestic Fuel Oil:		
Gasolene: (Kilotonnes)		

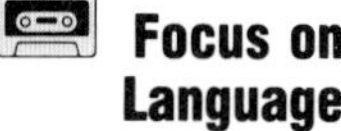
Check your
chart in the key.

Focus on Language

Listen to the conversation again and write down the phrases that correspond to the list of purposes. Some have been done as examples.

PHRASE	PURPOSE
1 ____________________	Lewis is informally asking about Hanna and the situation in general.
2 *What's the weather like...?*	He is asking whether it is good, bad, etc.

3 *You've got some figures for me?*	He makes a question only by using intonation, showing that he is expecting confirmation.
4 ______________________________	Hanna is telling him what kind of information she is going to give.
5 ______________________________	Lewis uses this phrase to show he is ready, and that she should start.
6 *We'd figured on 220 KT for heavy fuel oil....*	She is re-affirming the forecast figure,...
7 ______________________________	...and giving the latest information.
8 ______________________________	Hanna is showing she agrees with what Lewis has said.
9 ______________________________	Hanna is explaining that the reason for the change is the weather.
10 ______________________________	Lewis wants to know if the situation will change even more.
11 ______________________________	Hanna is saying she doesn't have a very definite opinion.
12 ______________________________	Lewis suggests having a final check of the estimates.
13 *We'll be in touch.*	This is an informal way of saying goodbye – it promises another contact without specifying when.

Check your answers in the key.

PRACTICE 1 Read the following sentences and choose the best answers.

1 *What's the weather like?*	Yes, I do. Raining.
2 *How're things?*	Fine, thanks. And you? I don't think so.
3 *The figure for January was 68K, wasn't it?*	It's right. That's right.
4 *Shall we run over those figures again?*	Yes, let's. Yes, we shall.
5 *Is there anything else?*	That's all. Anything.
6 *Please call me again next month.*	OK, I will. OK, I do.

Check your answers in the key.

PRACTICE 2 **Pronunciation**

Listen to the next part of the cassette and repeat the phrases, without the aid of the book.

Then listen and repeat with the book, or after having looked at it.

PHRASE	NOTES
1 *How're things?*	
2 *What's it like in London?*	
3 *You've got some figures for me?*	The rising intonation makes this into a question.
4 *Go ahead.*	
5 *We'd figured on 220 KT for heavy fuel oil.*	
6 *That's a drop of 20 KT.*	
7 *Why is that?*	
8 *There's been a sharp increase recently in the use of other energy sources.*	
9 *150 KT!*	Strong intonation showing surprise.

10 *Let's run over those estimates again.*

11 *We'll be in touch.*

Language Summary

This section draws attention to some of the language used in the dialogue.

	EXAMPLE	COMMENT
Past perfect tense	*We'd figured on 220 KT.*	Before the latest estimates.
Present perfect tense	*There's been a sharp increase in the use of other energy sources.*	Recently, i e from not long ago in the past up until the present.
Have got	*You've got some figures for me?* *I've got our best estimates for January.* *I've got the forecast in front of me.* *Have you got anything new there?*	U.S. English uses *have* where U.K. English tends to use *have got.*
Due to (cause and effect)	*This is due to the cold weather we've been having.*	It means *because of.*

PART 2

This part of the unit gives you further practice in using the language presented in Part 1.

ACTIVITY 1

Look at the following table. Answer your sales department colleague's questions, using the information in the table.

Month FEBRUARY	*Forecast*	*Best Estimate*	*Reason*
Price Unit raw material:	$50	$70	Bad weather
Production:	5,000 units	4,000 units	Strike by machine room operators

Compare your version with the model version in the key. It is on the cassette.

ACTIVITY 2 Look at the following graph. Answer another colleague's questions, using the information on the graph.

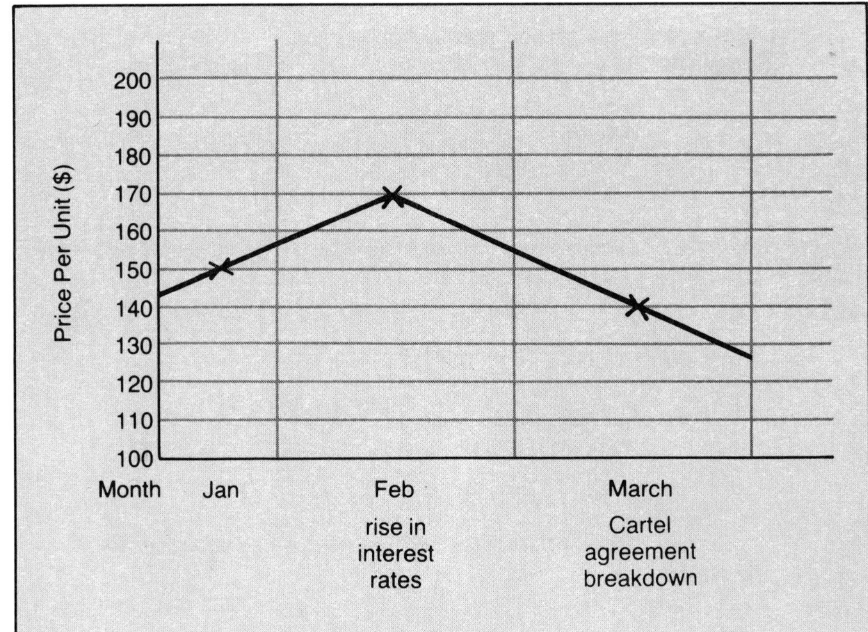

Compare your version with the model version in the key. It is on the cassette.

ACTIVITY 3 Look at the following balance sheet for an ice cream manufacturing company. Now look at the temperature chart on the opposite page. Answer a market researcher's questions, giving a reason for the changes.

Month	*Income*	*Expenditure*
June	$100,000	$80,000
July	$110,000	$90,000
August	$200,000	$120,000
September	$150,000	$100,000

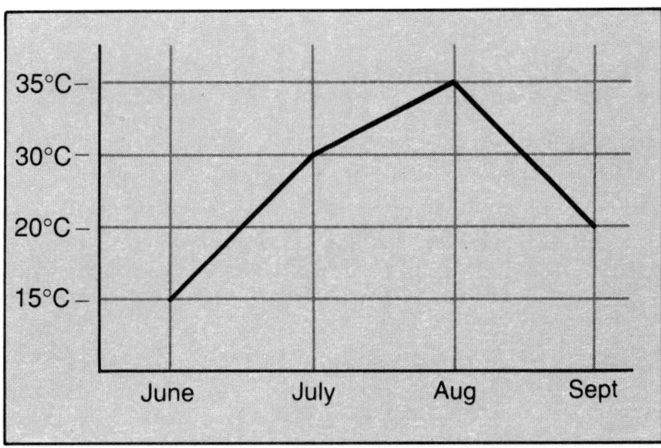

Compare your version with the model version in the key. It is on the cassette.

ACTIVITY 4 Ask your colleague questions to find out the twelve month inflation figures which are recorded for each of the months from September to December. You will hear the information you need to complete the chart. You should also try to find a reason for the trend.

Month:	SEPT.	OCT.	NOV.	DEC.
Inflation % :				

Compare your version with the model version in the key. It is on the cassette.

Glossary

forecasts	predictions, in this case about future figures
counterpart	equivalent worker in another branch
affiliates	branches of a company
update	to give the latest information
estimate	an approximate figure
best estimate	the latest approximate figure
figure on	to forecast
run over	to check
strike	a period of non-activity, when people refuse to work for a specific reason
cartel	an international group of companies which agree on the control of price and output

7 Participating in a telephone conference

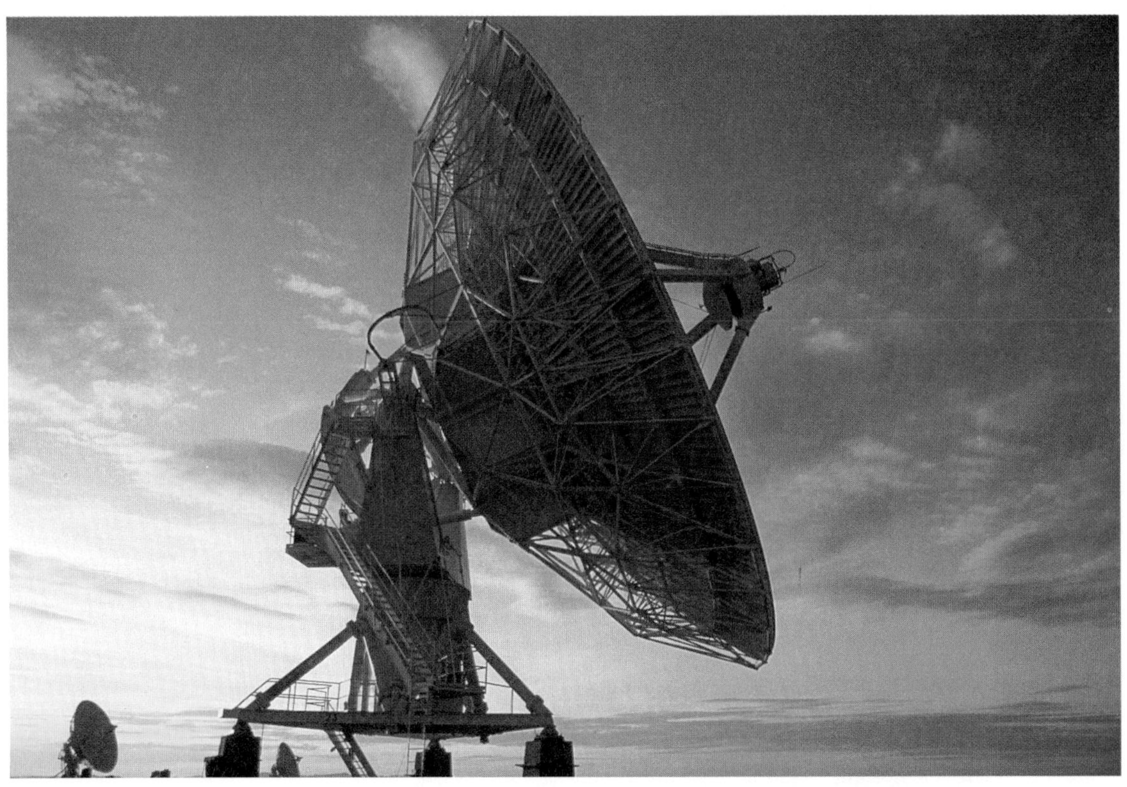

PART 1

This unit looks at the new but increasingly important field of telephone conferences. In this case you are going to hear a multi-participant telephone conversation. The telephone conference link used here allows the Head Office of a company to keep in regular touch with a team working on a computerized project in one of the company's subsidiaries.

Background

A major computerized system which was recently set up in the subsidiary has run into difficulty. The lapses in response times at peak operational periods have meant unacceptably long waiting periods in a highly mechanized industry. The purpose of these regular contact meetings is to try to improve the system and to monitor all operations, which take place on a networked computer system. The participants are sitting around a console which contains both microphones and loudspeakers. The structure is identical in both the Headquarters and the subsidiary.

Listening for information

While you are listening:

1 Mark the names of the participants in the correct place on the console.

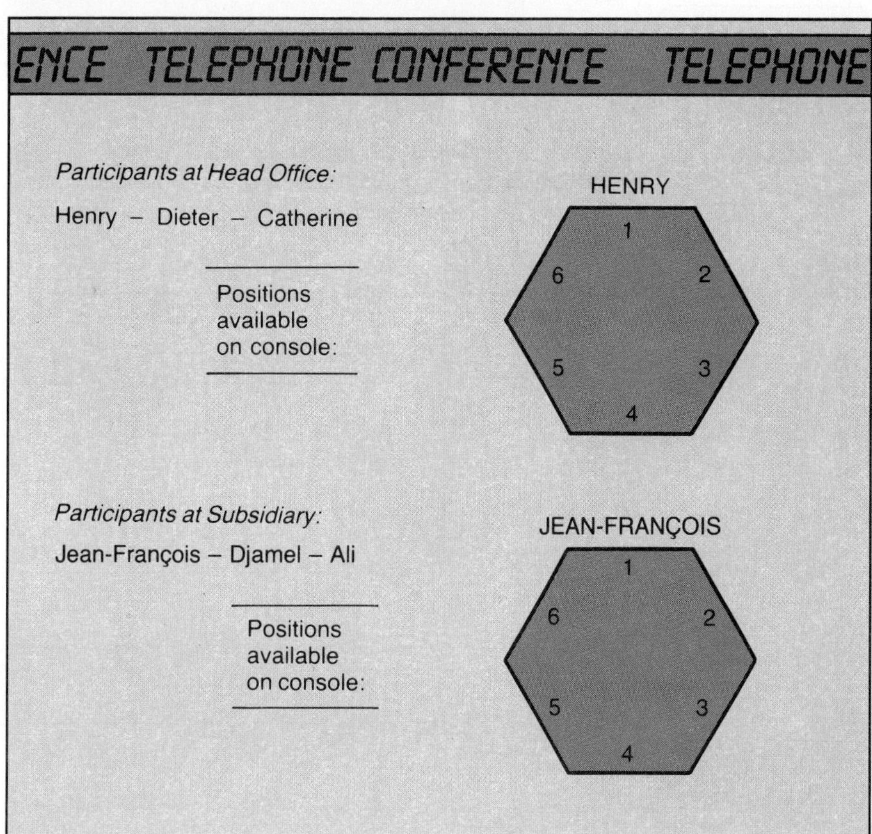

All the participants have a list on the console in front of them on which they can write the names of the corresponding participants. This is how the system works: as each person speaks, a light shows on the counterparts' console showing which position the voice is coming from.

2 Write the names in the appropriate place on the list Henry has in front of him: then indicate who the first speaker was.

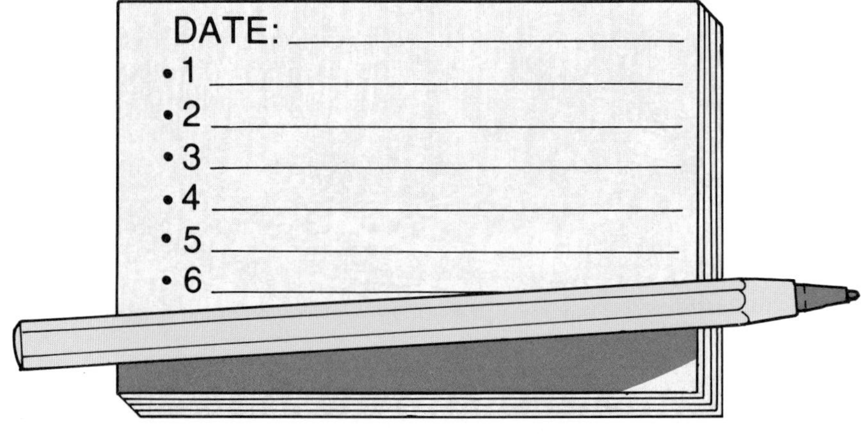

Check your answers in the key.

3 At the beginning of the telephone meeting, the subsidiary sent a graph to Head Office by telefax. Listen to the cassette and complete the graph, shown here, with the correct figures.

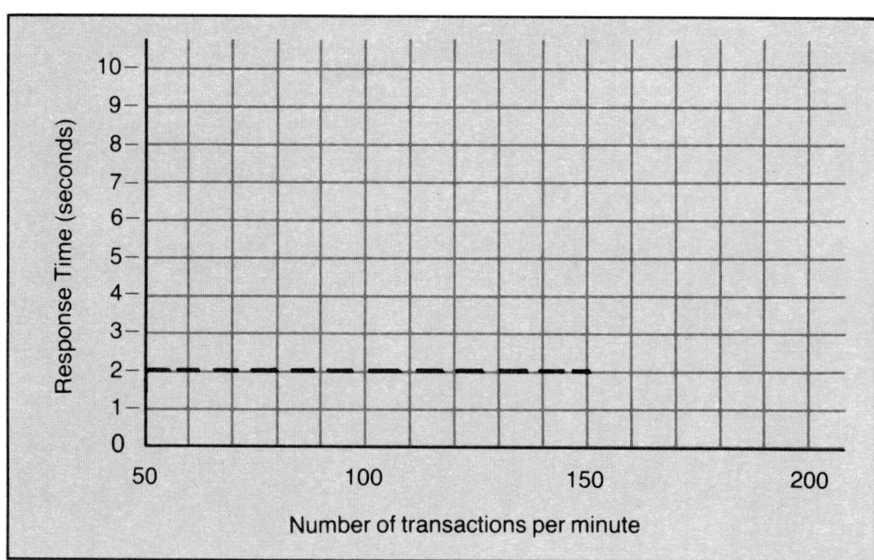

Check with the graph in the key.

4 Listed below are a number of statements that are supposed to be accurate reports of things Henry and Jean-François said. Some are accurate and some are inaccurate.

- Find the original statement in each case.
- Decide whether it is accurate or inaccurate.
- If it is inaccurate, make the changes needed to correct it.

a Henry says that the reception (from the subsidiary) is good.
b Jean-François introduces two colleagues called Ali and Djamel.
c Henry says that Catherine James has come in as a consultant on this meeting only.
d Henry says that the telefax shows the problems resulting from using the system heavily at certain times.
e Henry says that what they need to do is to make the system work faster.
f Henry says he's going to think about the problem between now and next week and come back with an answer.

Check your answers in the key.

CHECKLIST The following are all important elements in the conduct of a telephone conference. Which of them were present on the cassette?

	Yes	*No*
1 Use clear visual aids	☐	☐
2 Have a leader	☐	☐
3 Have an agenda if possible	☐	☐
4 Start with introductions	☐	☐
5 Speak one at a time	☐	☐

Now justify your *Yes/No* answer.

1 If you said *Yes* give an example of a visual aid.
2 If you said *Yes*, who is it?
3 If you said *Yes*, what is the agenda?
4 If you said *Yes*, give an example.
5 If you said *No*, give an example.

Check your answers in the key.

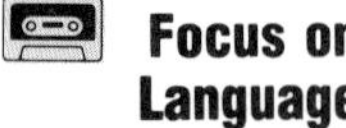

Focus on Language

Listen to the conversation again and write down phrases that correspond to the list of purposes below. Two have been done already.

PHRASE	PURPOSE
1 *Can you all hear us?*	The first caller is checking that the reception is good.
2 ______	How does Henry show that everything is in order?
3 ______	This is how Jean-François introduces himself.
4 ______	Henry introduces Catherine quite formally: what does he say?
5 *Good morning to everybody.*	Jean-François is generally greeting everyone.
6 ______	Catherine interrupts to ask about the graph.
7 ______	Jean-François is suggesting their next meeting date.
8 ______	Jean-François is saying goodbye.

Language Summary

This section draws attention to some of the language used in the dialogue.

	EXAMPLE	COMMENT
Can	*Can I start by asking if you have received the copies?*	
	Can I come in here to ask a question?	*Can I* is a rather neutral way of interrupting.
How	*How frequently do you make that number of transactions?*	*How* is followed directly by the adverb in this question.
	How does that sound?	This is an informal way of asking for an opinion.
Let	*Let me just say who is here today.*	This is an informal way of starting this introduction.

PRACTICE

Pronunciation

Listen to the next part of the cassette and repeat the phrases, without the aid of the book. Then listen and repeat with the book, or after having looked at it.

PHRASE

1. *Let me just say who is here today.*
2. *There is myself.*
3. *I'd like to introduce Catherine James.*
4. *Good morning to everybody.*
5. *That's right.*
6. *Exactly.*
7. *Can I come in here to ask a question?*
8. *How does that sound?*
9. *That's fine with us.*
10. *Until next week.*

PART 2

This part of the unit gives you the opportunity to practise introducing people on the phone, and also to improve the speed and clarity of your speech.

ACTIVITY 1

In this activity, your aim is to speak at the same speed as a native speaker. You can do this by reading the following text as you listen to the cassette – but it is not a repetition exercise, you read at the same time. You can also try reading it aloud in the same amount of time as the cassette.

Hello, this is ABC in Southampton, and we're receiving you loud and clear, London. There are four of us here today; myself, Frances; Horst, who is on my left; on his left is Pierre; and Joanna who is on my right. We have copies of the agenda, so go ahead please, London.

ACTIVITY 2

Look at the diagram of a teleconference console. You are the leader of the meeting; open by introducing your colleagues to the other participants in the meeting.

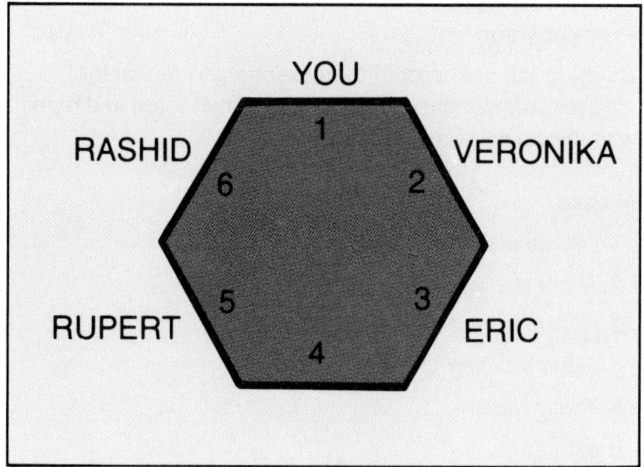

Compare your version with the model version in the key. It is on the cassette.

ACTIVITY 3

Listen to the extract on your cassette. When Henry asks the question, Jean-François and Ali both want to answer and they start speaking at the same time. The following sentences would all be good responses here: but which ones did they actually use?

a *Perhaps I could answer that.*
b *If I could just come in here.*
c *I think I may have the answer to that.*
d *I'd like to say something on that.*

This is a slightly embarrassing situation. What would you say to get out of it and to invite the other person to speak?

Check your suggestions with the key.

ACTIVITY 4 Choose the right answer.

Switchboard Hello, Victoria Holdings.

Client Hello, (1) *could/would* I speak to Bob Delonn, please?

Switchboard It's engaged (2) *will/shall* you hold?

Client Yes, I'll (3) *hold/keep* on.

(Pause)

Switchboard Hello caller? Are you (4) *yet/still* (5) *here/there*?

Client Yes.

Switchboard Sorry to (6) *wait/keep* you. It's (7) *ringing/calling* for you now.

Client Thank you.

Bob Delonn Bob Delonn speaking.

Client Hello, (8) *this/I* (9) *is/am* Barbara Michaels. I'm calling (10) *for/about* our meeting.

Bob Delonn I'm afraid I (11) *can't/won't* be able to (12) *make/do* it.

Client (13) *It's/That's* a shame.

Bob Delonn Yes, I'm (14) *afraid/sorry* something else has come up at the last minute.

Client Well, (15) *actually/indeed,* it (16) *suits/convenient* me if we can (17) *do/make* it another day.

Bob Delonn (18) *For me/As far as I'm concerned,* it'd be better to put it off for another week.

(19) *Are/Do* you agree?

Client (20) *I'll/I* get my diary and have a look. Yes, (21) *that's/it's* fine.

Bob Delonn Good. My colleague Franco Leone would like to have a quick word with you. Do you have a moment?

Client Yes, sure.

Bob Delonn OK, I'll put (22) *him to you through/him through to you* now, and I'll look (23) *towards/forward to* our meeting.

Client Goodbye.

Bob Delonn Goodbye.

Glossary

to keep in touch	to stay in contact
team	a group of people working together
computerized	controlled by a computer
subsidiary	a branch connected to the main company
lapse	a short period of time where nothing happens
response time	the time it takes to get a desired result, or an answer
peak	the highest point (here, the busiest)
to monitor	to follow closely, pay attention to
console	a flat surface containing the controls for a machine
loudspeaker	the part of a sound system that sends out sound
telefax	(abbr. telefacsimile), a message produced on paper and sent by wires to be reproduced in the same form at the receiving end
to put something off	to postpone, make a later date than originally planned

Key: Tapescript and answers

UNIT 1 TAPESCRIPT AND ANSWERS

Conversation

Switchboard operator Rider House, good morning.

Steve Newman Good morning. I'd like to speak to someone about renting office space, please.

Switchboard operator I'll put you through to Victoria Holdings. They're the people that deal with it. Just a moment.

Steve Newman Thank you.

Switchboard operator The number's engaged. Will you hold?

Steve Newman Yes, I'll hold on.

Switchboard operator Hello caller, the number's ringing for you now.

Steve Newman Thank you.

Administrative assistant Victoria Holdings, can I help you?

Steve Newman Yes, I'm interested in renting office space in Central London.

Administrative assistant Yes, for what size company?

Steve Newman It's a small company of about ten people.

Administrative assistant And what type of activity?

Steve Newman Insurance selling.

Administrative assistant Could I have the name of the company, please?

Steve Newman Yes, it's McGraw Continental.

Administrative assistant Could you spell that name for me, please?

Steve Newman	Yes, it's M.C.G.R.A.W.
Administrative assistant	And may I have your name?
Steve Newman	Yes, my name is Steve Newman.
Administrative assistant	And your number?
Steve Newman	01-449-8927.
Administrative assistant	449-8927. I'll pass this information on to Mr Michael Green who will be able to help you. Can he ring you back within the next hour?
Steve Newman	Yes, certainly. May I have your name, please?
Administrative assistant	Yes, of course. It's Charles Hughes. I'll get Michael Green to call you back and thank you for your call.

Listening for information

Victoria Holdings Ltd
Memo
Date
To Michael Green
Steve Newman of McGraw Continental called
Time Morning
Caller's number is
01-449-8927
Message
Please ring him with regards renting office space.
From Charles Hughes

Focus on Language

2 *I'll put you through to. . .*

4 *Will you hold?*

5 *Yes, I'll hold on.*

6 *the number's ringing for you now.*

9 *Could you spell that name for me, please?*

11 *I'll pass this information on. . .*

12 *Can he ring you back. . .?*

PRACTICE 1

1 it is

2 This is

3 I'm calling

4 Will you hold?

5 Yes, I will.

6 Could

7 I'll ask

8 back

ACTIVITY 1

Switchboard Zanek Computers.

You I'd like to speak to someone about your Triple X microcomputers.

Switchboard I'll put you through to our Sales Department. Hold the line, please.

You Thank you.

Switchboard The number's ringing for you now.

You Thank you.

ACTIVITY 2

Sales assistant Sales, can I help you?

You I'm interested in your Triple X microcomputers.

Sales assistant For use in the home or in the office?

You In the office.

Sales assistant Fine. Can I have the name of your company?

You Bartlett and Company.

Sales assistant Could you spell that for me, please?

You B.A.R.T.L.E.T.T.

Sales assistant Thank you. And your name?

You Helen Brown

Sales assistant And may I have your number?

You	927-5651
Sales assistant	Thank you. I'll ask our sales representative to call you back.

ACTIVITY 3

You	Hello, accounts?
Caller	Can I speak to Judith Roberts, please?
You	Her number's engaged, will you hold?
Caller	Yes, I'll hold on.
You	Thank you. It's ringing for you now.
Caller	Thank you.

ACTIVITY 4

You	Hello, sales.
Caller	Hello, I'm interested in your video cassette recorders.
You	Standard or Deluxe?
Caller	Deluxe.
You	May I have your name?
Caller	Yes, it's Catherine Stewart.
You	And the name of the company?
Caller	Nora G.B.
You	And your number?
Caller	96-39651
You	I'll pass this information on to Geoffrey White who will be able to help you.
Caller	Thank you.
You	Goodbye.
Caller	Bye.

UNIT 2 TAPESCRIPT AND ANSWERS

Message

Webster	This is Lionel Webster speaking. I'm not in the office at the moment but I expect to be back shortly. Please leave your name, number and a message of no more than three minutes when you hear the signal. Thank you for your call.
Bonner	Helmut Bonner here – that's B.O.N.N.E.R. I'm calling from Hamburg and my number is 880-51-01. I'm calling about our next delivery to you. The estimated day of arrival in Felixstowe is now 8th February. The vessel will be the "Atheco" – I'll spell that – A.T.H.E.C.O. She sails under

a Panamanian flag and her owner is the Greek Company, A & S Freightlines. I'll call back within the next two days with the exact time of arrival.

Listening for information

Name of caller: Bonner, Helmut

Callback number: 880-51-01

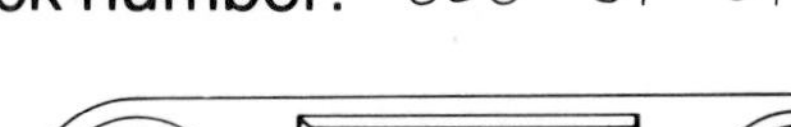

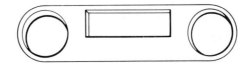

Estimated date of delivery: 8 Feb

Arrival port: Felixstowe

Name of vessel: Atheco

Owner: A + S Freightlines

Focus on Language

1 **a** *This is Lionel Webster speaking.*
  b *I'm not in the office at the moment. . .*
  c *Please leave your name, number and a message...*
  d *Thank you for your call.*

2 *be back shortly*

3 *Helmut Bonner here*

4 *that's. . .*
  I'll spell that. . .

5 *I'm calling about. . .*

6 *Within the next two days. . .*

7 *No.*

PRACTICE 2

This is Rachel Adams. I'm in a meeting at the moment but I'll be back at midday. Please leave your name, number and a message and I'll call you back, or you can try this afternoon. Thank you for your call.

ACTIVITY 1

a This is the Argentine Mining Confederation's Information Service. The Latin American Congress on Mining will be held in Mendoza, Argentina, between the 7th and 12th October 1987. The congress is sponsored by the Argentinian Government. For further details please write to Congresos Internacionales, Moreno 584, Buenos Aires 1091.

Organizer: Argentine Mining Confederation
Sponsor: Argentinian Government
Title of Congress: The Latin American Congress on Mining

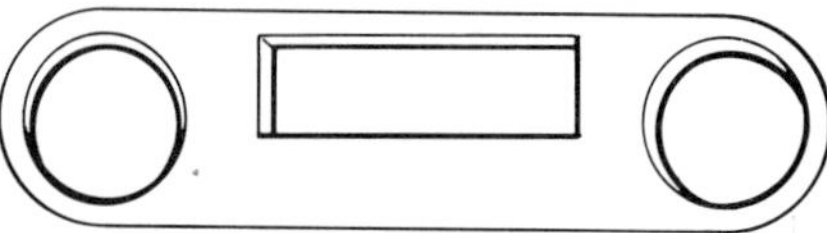

Place: Mendoza, Argentina
Date: 7 to 12 October, 1987
Address for further information: Congresos Internacionales Moreno 584, Buenos Aires 1091

b This is Kay Smith here. I'm coming to the Congress in Buenos Aires and will leave from Madrid on 5th of October. My flight number is AA 817, leaving at 20.05. I'll arrive at 08.05 on 6th October.

ACTIVITY 2 This is a recorded announcement from Charter Air on flights leaving Paris for New York, Boston and Philadelphia. Flight number 403 to JFK New York leaves at 13.20 on Sunday February 24th. We still have some places available on this flight.

We have very few seats left on flight 615 to Boston on Friday, 22nd February, leaving Paris Charles de Gaulle at 18.30. Flight 547 to Philadelphia is fully booked: if you have reservations, please call at our offices to collect your tickets. Thank you.

	1	2	3
Destination	New York	Boston	Philadelphia
Flight number	403	615	547
Date of departure	24 February	22 February	—
Time of departure	13.20	18.30	—
Availability of places	Fair	A few seats left	Fully booked

ACTIVITY 3 Check your version with the message by Rachel Adams in Part 1, Practice 2, of this unit.

UNIT 3 TAPESCRIPT AND ANSWERS

Conversation

Secretary Hello, Wool Touch.

Mr Sanchez Can I speak to Ms Alexander, please?

Secretary Yes, who's calling, please?

Mr Sanchez It's Mr Sanchez of the General Union Bank.

Secretary And what is it about?

Mr Sanchez She rang me earlier. I am returning her call.

Secretary Just a moment please, Mr Sanchez.

Ms Alexander Hello, Mr Sanchez, thank you for calling me back so promptly.

Mr Sanchez Not at all. It was about credit facilities, wasn't it?

Ms Alexander Yes, that's right. I'd like to know more about the sort of services you offer.

Mr Sanchez And I believe you're planning on investing in new equipment. Is that right?

Ms Alexander Yes, it's part of our overall expansion drive.

Mr Sanchez Were you thinking in terms of overdraft facilities or a fixed loan?

Ms Alexander Well, I'm not sure which would be best.

Mr Sanchez You do realize that in either case we would charge you a commitment fee, don't you?

Ms Alexander No, I hadn't realized that.

Mr Sanchez Would you like to come in and see me to discuss the types of loan available as well as the conditions attached?

Ms Alexander Yes, I think that would be best. Can we fix an appointment now?

Mr Sanchez Yes, certainly. Let me get my diary. Does tomorrow morning suit you? That's the 10th.

Ms Alexander Yes, that's fine. What time?

Mr Sanchez Shall we say ten? And if you don't mind I'll ask Mr Peterson to be with us as well. He's my assistant and you may have to deal with him later. I'll just make a note of that.

Ms Alexander That's fine by me.

Mr Sanchez Good. I'll look forward to seeing you then. Goodbye.

Ms Alexander Goodbye.

Listening for information

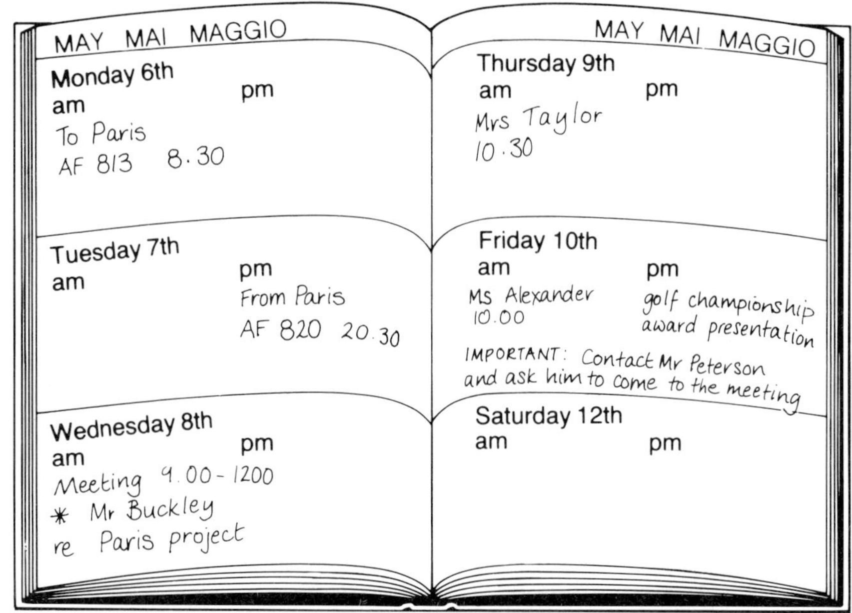

MAY MAI MAGGIO
Monday 6th
am
pm
To Paris
AF 813 8.30
Tuesday 7th
am
pm
From Paris
AF 820 20.30
Wednesday 8th
am
pm
Meeting 9.00-1200
* Mr Buckley
re Paris project
MAY MAI MAGGIO
Thursday 9th
am
pm
Mrs Taylor
10.30
Friday 10th
am
pm
Ms Alexander
10.00
golf championship
award presentation
IMPORTANT: Contact Mr Peterson
and ask him to come to the meeting
Saturday 12th
am
pm

Focus on Language

1 *It's Mr Sanchez of the General Union Bank.*

3 *She rang me earlier. I am returning her call.*

4 *Well, I'm not sure which would be best.*

8 *Let me get my diary.*

10 *Shall we say ten?*

11 *That's fine by me.*

PRACTICE 1

		Speaker
1	*wouldn't it?*	Alexander
2	*isn't it?*	Sanchez
3	*didn't they?*	Sanchez
4	*aren't you?*	Sanchez
5	*couldn't I?*	Alexander

PRACTICE 2

1 *As I understand it, the General Union Loan Scheme is designed to help small companies. Is that right?*

2 *I've been told a loan is more appropriate than an overdraft. Is that right?*

3 *I believe Wool Touch is expanding into the American market. Is that right?*

4 *I've heard that Wool Touch won a design award last year. Is that right?*

PRACTICE 3

A 1 *Shall we say Tuesday at the Commodore Hotel?*

2 *Shall we say 12% over 18 months?*

B **3** formal **4** informal
5 formal **6** informal

ACTIVITY 1

Helen Green Hello, Helen Green.
You Hello Helen, I'd like to arrange a meeting.
Helen Green Yes, when?
You What about Monday morning?
Helen Green Monday morning? That's OK. What time?
You Shall we say eleven?
Helen Green Eleven's fine. Bye now.
You Bye.

ACTIVITY 2

Rafael Hello, this is Rafael. I'm returning your call.
You Hello, I'd like to fix an appointment to see you.
Rafael Yes, certainly. When for?
You Let me get my diary. What about Wednesday morning?
Rafael Wednesday morning. OK. What time?
You Shall we say half past nine?
Rafael Half past nine suits me. Look forward to seeing you then. Bye.
You Bye.

ACTIVITY 3 Missing sentences from the conversation.

1 Speaking.

2 This is

3 Yes.

4 Would ten o'clock suit you? *or*
How about ten o'clock?

5 That's fine. *or*
That's okay with me.

6 See you then.

ACTIVITY 4

Sophie Weiss Hello, Sophie Weiss.

Tito Saronno Hello, this is Tito Saronno. I'd like some information about your insurance benefit schemes.

Sophie Weiss Yes, what exactly are you interested in?

Tito Saronno You do cover countries outside the U.K., don't you?

Sophie Weiss Yes, we specialize in people working abroad.

Tito Saronno And I believe you have group policies, don't you?

Sophie Weiss Yes, we do. I could send you our brochure if you like. Was it medical or pension you were interested in?

Tito Saronno Medical.

Sophie Weiss Right, I'll send something you can have a look at and if it's interesting just give me a ring. Can I have your name again and address?

Tito Saronno Yes, it's Tito Saronno, that's double 'n'.

Sophie Weiss Yes.

Tito Saronno And it's 30c via Turati, Milan.

Sophie Weiss Right. I'll put that in the post today.

Tito Saronno Thank you. Bye.

Sophie Weiss Goodbye.

The broker did **not** tick

☐ voluntary

☐ International Pensions

☐ Group Life

There was one mistake: the street number was not *36,* it was *30c.*

UNIT 4 TAPESCRIPT AND ANSWERS

Janine Berman Janine Berman.

Nils Ekström Hello, Janine, this is Nils Ekström calling from Sweden.

Janine Berman Ah, hello Nils. How are you?

Nils Ekström Oh, fine thanks. It's about our meeting – I'm afraid I won't be able to make it after all.

Janine Berman Oh dear. Would you like to arrange another date?

Nils Ekström Well, not immediately. You see, we're very busy here – but I have heard some interesting rumours about the new PAL.

Janine Berman Yes, well, I think we can say that the PAL *is* very promising even if the stock market is behaving a bit strangely.

Nils Ekström Hm – the market is bad at the moment – actually some people are saying the shares are too high.

Janine Berman I think that's understandable and – er – in fact the AGM in two weeks' time is going to be an excellent chance for the President to clarify things for shareholders.

Nils Ekström Well, actually I am coming to the AGM and I'll be bringing a client who is in fact quite a large shareholder.

Janine Berman Ah well, that's very interesting. I'll look forward to seeing you then and perhaps we could have a chat there instead.

Nils Ekström Yes, indeed. I'll look forward to it.

Listening for information

1 To explain he cannot come to the meeting.

2 He cancelled it.

3 Yes. *(behaving strangely – bad)*

4 No. *(the shares are too high)*

5 Yes, probably, because of the new PAL.

6 Yes.

7 No. He wanted to talk about the company's situation, as well.

Focus on Language

1 *It's about our meeting –*

2 *I'm afraid. . .*

4 *. . .the PAL is very promising even if the stock market is behaving a bit strangely.*

6 *Well, actually, I am coming. . .*

8 *Yes, indeed.*

PRACTICE 1

1 *Shall we make it 10 o'clock?*

2 *Let's make it Friday.*

3 *Could you make it next week?*

4 *I'm afraid I can't make the department meeting.*

5 *I'm sorry but I can't make the first appointment.*

6 *I won't be able to make Friday I'm afraid.*

ACTIVITY 1 REASONS WHY THEY ARE SIMILAR.

Numbers 1 and 6 mean *not available.*
Numbers 2 and 10 mean *not present.*
Numbers 3 and 9 mean *specifically not in.*
Numbers 4 and 7 mean *already busy.*
Numbers 5 and 8 mean *not available today.*

ACTIVITY 2

Patient 1 Can I speak to Dr Rogers, please?

You I'm afraid she'll be out all morning.

Patient 2 Could you put me through to Dr Lemon, please?

You I'm sorry, but he's with a patient.

Patient 3 I'd like to speak to Dr Willis.

You I'm sorry but she's on holiday.

Patient 4 Dr Morris, please.

You I'm afraid he's not in today.

Patient 5 Could I speak to Dr Poole, please?

You I'm sorry but she's not available at the moment.

Patient 6 Can I have Dr Nahri, please?

You I'm afraid he's sick today.

ACTIVITY 3

1 The 1984 French arms sales total was $6.66 bn. which was double the 1983 total. Indeed, it was a record.

2 In Europe, wages are linked to prices and unemployment grows. In Japan, wages are linked to company profits. In fact, unemployment is relatively insignificant.

3 Natural Grain Products started in 1970. Its president, Laurence Ford, is now a rich man. Actually, sales totalled $7 m. last year.

UNIT 5 TAPESCRIPTS AND KEY

Employee 6824

Josephine Pinzan Is that the restaurant?

Employee No, it isn't. You've got the wrong extension. The restaurant is 6428. Just a minute. I'll see if I can put you through.

Josephine Pinzan Thank you, sorry to trouble you.

Ingrid Bellini Mrs Bellini.

Josephine Pinzan	Hello, this is Josephine Pinzan, I'm the new Press Officer.
Ingrid Bellini	Sorry, I didn't catch your surname.
Josephine	Pinzan. P.I.N.Z.A.N.
Ingrid Bellini	Oh yes, now I recognize it. How can I help you Mrs Pinzan?
Josephine Pinzan	I'd like to book a room for lunch next Thursday. I've got some people from Associated Press coming.
Ingrid Bellini	I'm afraid this is a bad line. What day did you say?
Josephine Pinzan	Thursday. For lunch. We'll be six or seven. I'll let you know definitely later on.
Ingrid Bellini	I'm sorry but could you repeat how many? I'm afraid it really *is* a bad line.
Josephine Pinzan	Six or seven. I'll have to confirm it.
Ingrid Bellini	And what kind of menu would you like?
Josephine Pinzan	Nothing particularly special – what do you suggest?
Ingrid Bellini	Our regular menu, then – we normally offer a starter followed by a main course and salad, cheese and a dessert.
Josephine Pinzan	Could you run through the choices?
Ingrid Bellini	Yes, you could have fish or meat as a main course, then soufflé, ice cream or pie for dessert.
Josephine Pinzan	Sorry, soufflé, ice cream or. . .?
Ingrid Bellini	Pie. We'll have a choice of two or three to offer you.
Josephine Pinzan	Could I think about it and call you back?
Ingrid Bellini	Yes, please do.
Josephine Pinzan	You did say Thursday was all right, didn't you?
Ingrid Bellini	I'll check my bookings but I'm pretty sure it is.
Josephine Pinzan	I'll let you have the details as soon as possible.
Ingrid Bellini	Thank you, goodbye.
Josephine Pinzan	Goodbye.

Listening for information

1 She confused the numbers in the extension number.
2 Yes, she had.
3 The line was very faint at that point.
4 Seven
5 Something more formal.
6 The number of people and the day.

Focus on Language

1 *You've got the wrong extension.*
3 *Sorry to trouble you.*

4 *I didn't catch your surname.*

6 *What day did you say?*

8 *Could you repeat how many?*

10 *Could you run through the choices?*

11 *Sorry, soufflé, ice cream or . .?*

13 *Yes, please do.*

14 *You did say Thursday was all right, didn't you?*

16 *I'll let you have the details as soon as possible.*

ACTIVITY 1

Bonnard Hello? Bonnard speaking.

You Hello, is that Mr Bonner?

Bonnard Sorry. Mr who?

You Mr Bonner.

Bonnard Could you spell that?

You B.O.N.N.E.R.

Bonnard No, this is Mr Bonnard. What extension did you want?

You 5410

Bonnard This is 5019. I'll put you back to the switchboard and they'll connect you.

You Thank you.

ACTIVITY 2

Bassett Hello, James Bassett.

Stott Hello Mr Bassett. Simon Stott here – I'd like to ask whether you'd be interested in seeing your products more widely available to potential customers.

Bassett Sorry, what did you say your name was?

Stott Simon Stott, that's S.T.O.T.T., sales director. We deal with sophisticated firms such as yourselves and can offer you the possibility of wider exposure for your products than you're probably getting already.

Bassett So it's about advertising, is it?

Stott Yes, but I should point out that as specialists ourselves we can put you in touch with the kind of customer you're aiming your products at, through our review.

Bassett Could you give me the name of your review?

Stott Yes, it's *The Advertiser* and we have a circulation in your area alone of 45,000.

Bassett So, it's *The Advertiser* and – what did you say the circulation was?

Stott 45,000 but that's just in your immediate area.

Bassett Okay, Mr Stott, I'll have a word with our advertising manager and I expect he'll be in touch. Can you leave a phone number?

Stott Yes, it's 440 2882.

Bassett Okay. Goodbye.

Stott Bye.

Essential details

Simon Stott
Sales director for *The Advertiser*
Circulation: 45,000
Telephone number: 440 2882

ACTIVITY 3

Brian Williams Hello? Brian speaking.

You Hello, this is James.

Brian Williams Hello James, what can I do for you?

You Do you know *The Advertiser*?

Brian Williams *The Advertiser*? No, I'm afraid I don't know it.

You I just had a call from Simon Stott, their sales director.

Brian Williams Sorry? What was the name?

You Simon Stott, S.T.O.T.T.

Brian Williams S.T.O.T.T. Okay.

You He tells me the circulation figure is 45,000.

Brian Williams 55,000 – not bad!

You Not 55,000–45,000.

Brian Williams Oh, 45,000. Still. . .

You Could you phone him? The number is 440 2882.

Brian Williams 440 28. . .?

You 2882.

Brian Williams Okay, I'll give him a ring.

You Goodbye.

Brian Williams Bye.

ACTIVITY 4

1 *Caller* The name of the person I want is Delanya.
You Sorry, could you repeat the name?

2 *Caller* I'd like to come and see you at 11.45.
You Sorry, what time did you say?

3 *Caller* Could I leave a message for Mr D'Arcangelo?

	You	Sorry, Mr who?
4	*Caller*	I'd like to speak to Mrs Dalzell on 5801.
	You	Sorry, I didn't catch the number.
5	*Caller*	I'd like to make an appointment for Mrs Zehnacker.
	You	Could you spell the name?

UNIT 6 TAPESCRIPT AND KEY

Hanna Willems	Hello Lewis, Hanna here.
Lewis Brown	Hello Hanna, how're things? What's the weather like in Amsterdam?
Hanna Willems	A bit cold, what's it like in London?
Lewis Brown	Same, I'm afraid. You've got some figures for me?
Hanna Willems	Yes, I've got our best estimates for January.
Lewis Brown	OK, I've got the forecast in front of me. Go ahead.
Hanna Willems	We'd figured on 220 KT for heavy fuel oil but our best estimate of this is now 200 KT.
Lewis Brown	That's a drop of 20 KT.
Hanna Willems	Right.
Lewis Brown	Why is that?
Hanna Willems	There's been a sharp increase recently in the use of other energy sources.
Lewis Brown	The forecast for domestic fuel is 450 KT. Have you got anything new there?
Hanna Willems	Yes, our best estimate is now 500 KT.
Lewis Brown	That's an increase of 50 KT.
Hanna Willems	Yes, in fact this is due to the cold weather we've been having.
Lewis Brown	Is the situation likely to change?
Hanna Willems	It's hard to say. It could.
Lewis Brown	The forecast for gasolene was 180 KT.
Hanna Willems	180 KT, that's right. Our best estimate on that is now 150 KT.
Lewis Brown	150 KT!
Hanna Willems	This is down because of a delay in official price adjustment.
Lewis Brown	Let's run over those estimates again: heavy fuel oil – 200, domestic fuel oil – 500, gasolene – 150.
Hanna Willems	OK.
Lewis Brown	Good, we'll be in touch. Goodbye now.
Hanna Willems	Bye.

Listening for information

Month: JANUARY	Forecast	Best Estimate
Heavy Fuel Oil:	220 kt	200 kt
Domestic Fuel Oil:	450 kt	500 kt
Gasolene: (Kilotonnes)	180 kt	150 kt

Focus on Language

1 *How're things?*

4 *I've got our best estimates for January.*

5 *Go ahead.*

7 *Our best estimate of this is now 200 KT.*

8 *Right.*

9 *This is due to the cold weather we've been having.*

10 *Is the situation likely to change?*

11 *It's hard to say. It could.*

12 *Let's run over those estimates again.*

PRACTICE 1

1 Raining.
2 Fine, thanks.
3 That's right.
4 Yes, let's.
5 That's all.
6 OK, I will.

ACTIVITY 1

Colleague And what is your forecast price per unit of raw material for February?

You $50.

Colleague And your current best estimate?

You Well, that's $70.

Colleague Why the increase?

You Well, it's due to the bad weather.

Colleague What about the production forecast for February?

You 5,000 units.

Colleague And your current best estimate?

You That's 4,000 units.

Colleague Why the drop?

You Well, I'm afraid, it's because of a strike by machine room operators.

ACTIVITY 2

Colleague Tell me, what was the price per unit in January?
You $150.
Colleague And what about February?
You $170.
Colleague Oh, why the rise?
You Well, this was because of an increase in interest rates.
Colleague And what was the March figure?
You $140.
Colleague Why that's a big drop! What was the reason?
You The cartel agreement broke down.

ACTIVITY 3

Researcher What were the income and expenditure figures for June?
You $100,000 and $80,000.
Researcher And July?
You $110,000 and $90,000.
Researcher What about August?
You $200,000 and $120,000.
Researcher Good! And in September?
You $150,000 and $100,000.
Researcher What was the reason for the sharp increase?
You Well, as you might imagine, this was due to a very hot summer.

ACTIVITY 4

You What was the 12 month figure for inflation in September?
Caller 9.1%
You And October?
Caller 9.5%
You What about November?
Caller 10%
You And December?
Caller 10.7%
You I see. Have you any idea about the reason for the increase?
Caller Yeah, it was almost certainly because of an increase in interest rates.

UNIT 7 TAPESCRIPT AND KEY

Subsidiary Hello, can you all hear us?

Head Office Yes, you're coming through loud and clear.

Subsidiary Let me just say who is here today – there's myself, Jean-François, and on my left I have Djamel (Hello.) and on his left is Ali. (Hello.) Djamel and Ali are two of the trainees working with this system.

Head Office Thanks, Jean-François. At headquarters we've got myself, Henry, then next to me on my left is Dieter (Hello.) from Operations, whom you all know, and on my right I'd like to introduce Catherine James who's from our computer department and will be working with us as a consultant from now on. (Good morning.)

Jean-François Good morning to everybody. Can I start by asking if you have received the copies we sent through?

Henry Yes we have – the graph of peak period response times.

Jean-François That's right. You can see the problem.

Henry Yes, the response time goes shooting up to 10 seconds once you get past 150 transactions – it leaps from 2 right up to 10 seconds between 150 and 200 transactions.

Jean-François Exactly.

Henry And presumably the curve would keep going up like that.

Catherine James Can I come in here to ask a question – how typical is this curve? How frequently do you make that number of transactions per minute?

Jean-François (to Ali & Djamel) What do you think?

Djamel Perhaps I can answer that. The peak periods are every work day from 8 to 12 and from 2 to 6.

Henry We must do something to reduce these response times. I'd like to suggest that we go away and discuss the problem with Catherine and meet again next week. How does that sound?

Jean-François That's fine with us. Same time same day?

Henry Yes. Same time same day. We'll come back with some suggestions.

Jean-François Thanks, until next week, goodbye.

Henry & Catherine Goodbye.

Listening for information

1

HENRY

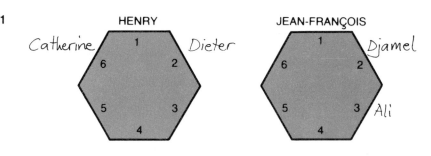

Catherine 1 Dieter
6 2
5 3
4

JEAN-FRANÇOIS

1 Djamel
6 2
5 3 Ali
4

2

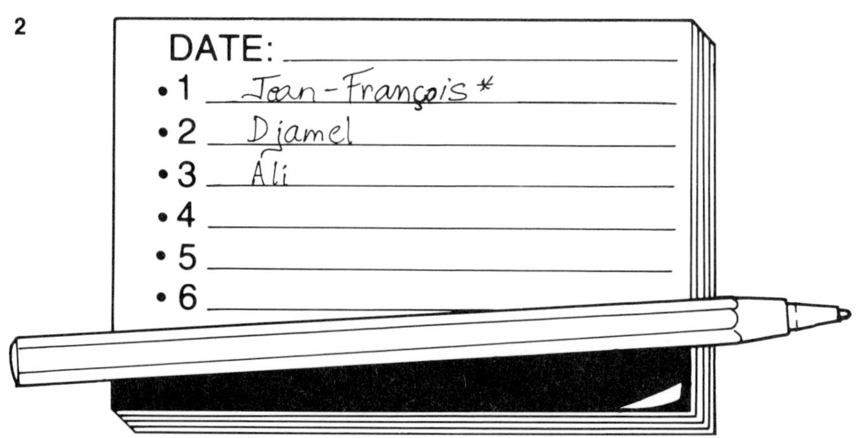

3

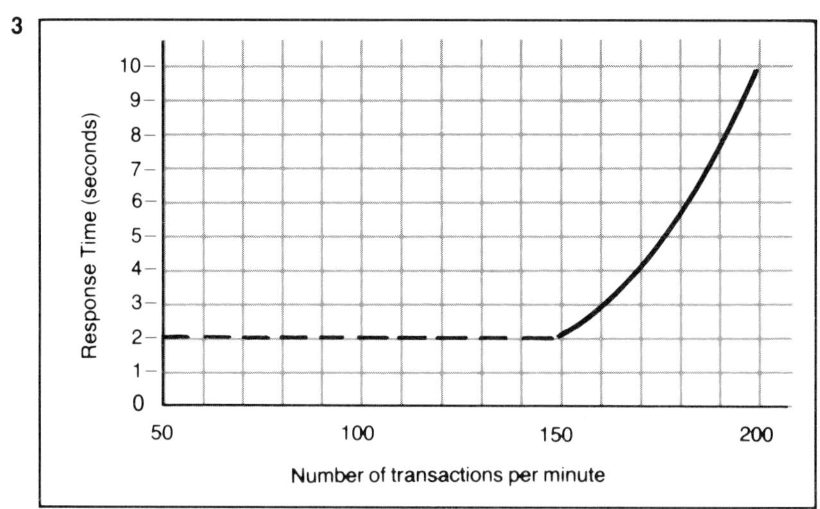

4 **a** Yes – *Loud and clear*
b No – *they are trainees*
c No – *(she) will be working with us as a consultant from now on.*
d Yes – *the graph of peak period response times*

e Yes – *we must do something to reduce those response times.*

f No – *I'd like to suggest that we go away and discuss the problem with Catherine and meet again next week.*

CHECKLIST

1 Yes	**1** the fax graph
2 Yes	**2** Jean-François
3 No	**2** No agenda
4 Yes	**4** eg *on my left I have Djamel.*
5 Yes	**5** They never speak together.

Focus on Language

2 *You're coming through loud and clear.*

3 *There's myself, Jean-François . . .*

4 *I'd like to introduce Catherine James. . .*

6 *Can I come in here to ask a question?*

7 *Same time same day?*

8 *Until next week, goodbye.*

ACTIVITY 2

There are five of us here today. Myself, Kay, then on my left is Veronika and on her left is Eric. Rashid is on my right and Rupert is on his right.

ACTIVITY 3

Henry This is Henry again. I'd like to ask a question about the jump up to 200. Why is it so sudden?
(At same time – Jean-François & Ali)

Jean-François If I could just come in here.

Ali Perhaps I could answer that.

Suggested ways of inviting the other to speak:
Sorry – you first. *or*
Please – go ahead.

ACTIVITY 4

CHECKLIST

1 could	**2** will	**3** hold
4 still	**5** there	**6** keep
7 ringing	**8** this	**9** is
10 about	**11** won't	**12** make
13 that's	**14** afraid	**15** actually
16 suits	**17** make	**18** as far as I'm concerned
19 do	**20** I'll	**21** that's
22 him through to you	**23** forward to	

Glossary

This glossary of telephoning terms is designed to provide you with a brief guide to the terms in current use, most of which you have already found in this book. They are grouped according to headings which signify the use you may make of them.

Introducing yourself

This is *(name).*
(name) speaking.
It's *(name).*
My name is. . .

Asking for someone or for a number

Is that *(name or number)*?
Could I speak to *(name)*? Can I speak to *(name)*?
It's *(name)*, isn't it?

Speaking with a switchboard operator

Can you put me through to *(name or number)*?
Can I have extension *(number)*?
I'd like to speak to *(name).*

Being helpful

You're through, caller – please go ahead.
The line's ringing for you, caller.
You're welcome. (*As a response to* thank you.)

Saying why you're calling

I'm calling about (the meeting).
I'm calling for (some information).
I'm calling to (let you know I'll be late).

Asking the caller to wait

Could you hold on?
Will you hold or will you call back later?
Trying to connect you, please hold the line.

Apologising

Sorry to keep you.
I'm afraid the line's engaged.
I'm sorry but there's no reply.

Offering to take a message

Can I take a message?
Would you like to leave a message?
Can I ask who's calling?

Asking to leave a message

Could I leave a message?
Could you get her to call me?
Could you tell her I rang?

Promising action

I'll get her to call you back.
I'll give him your message.
I'll call you on Monday.
I'll check that for you now.
I'll put you through to someone else.

Asking for repetition

I didn't catch that. Could you repeat what you said?
Sorry, what was the name?
I'm afraid it's a bad line. Could you speak up?

Saying goodbye

Nice talking to you.
I'll speak to you tomorrow.
Look forward to hearing from you again soon.